Michael M. Dediu

From **Euclid** to **Edison** – revelries in the last 75 years

A chronological and photographic documentary

DERC Publishing House
Tewksbury (Boston), Massachusetts, U. S. A.

Copyright ©2019 by Michael M. Dediu

All rights reserved

Published and printed in the
United States of America
On the Great Seal of the United States are included:
E Pluribus Unum (Out of many, one)
Annuit Coeptis (He has approved of the undertakings)
Novus Ordo Seclorum (New order of the ages)

Library of Congress Control Number: 2018914876

Dediu, Michael M.

From Euclid to Edison – revelries in the last 75 years
A chronological and photographic documentary

ISBN-13: 978-1-939757-81-4

Preface

It is always a great pleasure to remember and celebrate great personalities, who significantly contributed to our civilization, looking from a recent perspective.

From the father of geometry Euclid, to the founder of modern bacteriology Koch, from the great painters Leonardo da Vinci, Michelangelo and Rembrandt, to the celebrated inventor Edison, from the famous pharaohs of Egypt and the 4,578 years old Great Pyramid of Giza, to the unforgettable first man on the Moon and the 24 years old Amazon, we have hundreds of distinguished people and events mentioned in this book.

Do you remember Cicero, Paracelsus, Rabelais, Galilei, Pascal, or Frost? They all will say "Hello!" to you from these pages.

Starting from 1943, in a chronological order, a variety of pertinent information about the numerous relevant personalities and important events, which took place during the history, are commemorated in the last 75 years. There are also many attractive and historic photographs, some of reproductions which we accumulated over the years – I want to thank my wife for her assistance.

This book brings a rainbow of practical information, and this will certainly enhance everybody's joie de vivre.

Michael M. Dediu, Ph. D.

Tewksbury (Boston), U. S. A., 6 January 2019

Paris in 2013: the south-east of la Tour Eiffel (1889, 324 m including the antenna at the top; without the antenna, it is 300 m), seen from Avenue Anatole France in Champ de Mars. It was the tallest manmade structure for 41 years, until the Chrysler Building (319 m) was built in New York in 1930. This Sun-facing side of the tower heats up, and the top moves as much as 18 cm away from the Sun. The Sun also causes the tower to grow about 15 cm. La Tour Eiffel weighs over 10,000 tons, has over 5 billions of lights, 108 stories, with 1,710 steps. The first platform is at 58 m; the 2nd platform is at 115 m, and the third platform is 279 m up.

Table of Contents

Preface 3

Chapter 1. 1943 - 1952 7

Chapter 2. 1953 - 1962 19

Chapter 3. 1963 - 1972 30

Chapter 4. 1973 - 1982 52

Chapter 5. 1983 - 1992 79

Chapter 6. 1993 - 2002 100

Chapter 7. 2003 - 2012 110

Chapter 8. 2013 - 2018 131

Bibliography 140

On 7th Avenue at West 57th Street, looking southwest: right: a classical building, which is tangent to the right, on W 57th St, to the American Fine Arts Society building (1892); left down: a beautiful building, opposite Carnegie Hall (to the left, across 7th Ave, 1891, concert hall with exceptional acoustics, architecture and performance history); left up: an impressive double skyscraper, with the southwest side on W 56th St.

Chapter 1. 1943 - 1952

1943 –

- 4 January – 300th anniversary of the birth of Sir Isaac Newton (4 Jan 1643 – 31 March 1727, aged 84.2), great English mathematician, astronomer, theologian, author and physicist.

UK, Cambridge, a bas-relief on the eastern wall of the western building of the Old Court (1451) of Queens' College (1448), University of Cambridge, 60 m east of the Mathematical Bridge (1749).

- 14 February – The important German mathematician David Hilbert passed away, aged 81 years and 22 days (23 Jan 1862 – 14 Feb 1943).

- 5 July - The failed Battle of Kursk becomes the last Nazi offensive on the Eastern Front.

- 6 November – The author was born in Iasi (325 km northeast of Bucharest, 850 km east of Vienna, 1,100 km north of Athens, 1,200 km southeast of Berlin, 1,200 km southwest of Moscow, 1,300 km northeast of Rome, 1,500 km south of Helsinki, 1,900 km east of Paris, 2,000 km southeast of London).

- 11 November – 25 years ago, in 1918, in Ferdinand Foch's own railway carriage, in the Forest of Compiègne, France, took place the signing of the Armistice (by Allies (represented by France and UK) and Germany), marking the end of World War I, on 11 November 1918.

28 November – 1 Dec: Tehran Conference between Franklin Roosevelt, Winston Churchill and Joseph Stalin agrees to launch Operation Overlord.

- 11 December - 100th anniversary of the birth of Heinrich Hermann Robert Koch (11 December 1843 – 27 May 1910, aged 66.4), German physician and microbiologist. As the founder of modern bacteriology, he identified the specific causative agents of tuberculosis, cholera, and anthrax, and gave experimental support for the concept of infectious disease.

- 500 years ago, in 1443, King Sejong the Great published the hangul, the native phonetic alphabet system for the Korean language, which is in use today.

- 400 years ago, in 1543, Copernicus published his theory that the Earth and the other planets revolve around the Sun.

1944 –

- 509 years ago, in 1435, Verrocchio was born (1435 – 1488, aged 53, leading Italian (from Florence) painter and sculptor, teacher of Leonardo da Vinci).

- 24 May – 100 years ago, in 1844, the first publicly funded telegraph line in the world — between Baltimore and Washington — sent demonstration message, starting the age of the telegraph.

- 1 – 22 July - the United Nations Monetary and Financial Conference (730 delegates from 44 Allied nations) at Bretton Woods (12 km west of Mount Washington (1917 m), 250 km north of Boston, USA) starts, establishing the International Monetary Fund and the World Bank. The Bretton Woods system worked for 27 years, until 1971.

Mount Washington Resort, Bretton Woods, New Hampshire, USA, where the United Nations Monetary and Financial Conference took place in July 1944.

- 300th anniversary of the birth of Antonio Stradivari (1644 – 1737, aged 93). He was a famous luthier from Cremona (60 km west of Virgilio (birthplace of the great Latin poet Vergilius, 15 Oct 70 BC – 21 Sep 19 BC, aged 50.9), 75 km southeast of Milano), north of river Po, in Lombardia, where Stradivari crafted for 81 years (from the age of 12 to 93) over 700 best violins, cellos, guitars and harps, cold Stradivarius. The first violin was ordered by a descendent of Lorenzo de' Medici (1 Jan 1449 – 8 April 1492, aged 43.2) in 1555, in a letter to Andrea Amati, 50, (c 1505 – c. 1578, aged c. 73), who was the first from the Amati family of luthiers, followed by Antonio and brother Girolamo, Niccolo, and Girolamo (Hieronymus II, 26 Feb 1649 - 21 Feb 1740, aged 5 days before 91).

- 23 August - Romania was liberated from the German occupation (started about 7 years) by the Soviet troops, and immediately started the Soviet Union occupation and control of Romania, which will continue for over 45 years.

1945 –

- 3 March – 100th anniversary of the birth of Georg Ferdinand Ludwig Philipp Cantor (3 March 1845 – January 6, 1918, aged 72.8), German mathematician, who created set theory, which has become a fundamental theory in mathematics. Cantor established the importance of one-to-one correspondence between the members of two sets, defined infinite and well-ordered sets, and proved that the real numbers are more numerous than the natural numbers. In fact, Cantor's method of proof of this theorem implies the existence of an "infinity of infinities". He defined the cardinal and ordinal numbers and their arithmetic. Cantor's work is of great philosophical interest, a fact of which he was well aware.

- 12 April - Death of the 32nd President of the United States, for 12.1 years, Franklin Delano Roosevelt (30 Jan 1882 - 12 April 1945, aged 63.2).

Harry S. Truman, 60.9, (8 May 1884 – 26 Dec 1972, aged 88.6) became the 33rd President of the United States, for 7.7 years, (12 April 1945 – 20 January 1953) upon the death of Franklin D. Roosevelt, after serving as Vice President. He used atomic bombs in Japan, left Stalin to control China and North Korea, implemented the Marshall Plan to rebuild the economy of Western Europe, and established the Truman Doctrine and NATO.

16 days later, on 28 April, Benito Mussolini died (29 July 1883 - 28 April 1945, aged 61.7, dictator of Italy for 22 years).

2 days after that, on 30 April, Adolf Hitler died (20 April 1889, Austria - 30 April 1945, Berlin, aged 56, dictator of Germany for 12 years).

- 6 August - The first atomic bomb is dropped by the U.S. military on Hiroshima (western Japan, 800 km southwest of Tokyo).

- 800 years ago, in 1145, Latin translations, after 325 years, of Algoritmi (circa 780 – c 850, in Baghdad, aged c 70, Persian scholar who produced works in mathematics (founder of algebra and algorithm), geography and astronomy) textbook on arithmetic (Algorithmo de Numero Indorum), which codified the various Indian numerals, and introduced the decimal positional number system to the Western world. The Compendious Book on Calculation by Completion and Balancing, translated into Latin by Robert of Chester in 1145, was used for about 400 years, until the sixteenth century, as the principal mathematical text-book of European universities.

- 600 years ago, in 1345, the Cathedral Notre Dame de Paris, on the Île de la Cité was completed, after 182 years of construction.

- 500th anniversary of Sandro Botticelli's birth (1445 – 17 May 1510, aged 65, great Italian painter, 7 years older than Leonardo da Vinci).

- 400 years ago, in 1545, the theory of complex numbers was first developed by Gerolamo Cardamo of Italy.

- The microwave oven is patented in the U.S.

1946 –

- 1900 years ago, in 46, the historian Plutarch was born (46 – 120, aged 74).

- 10 January – The first meeting of the United Nations General Assembly opens in London.

1 July - 300th anniversary of the birth of Gottfried Wilhelm (von) Leibniz (1 July 1646 – 14 November 1716, aged 70.3) prominent German mathematician and philosopher in the history of mathematics and the history of philosophy. His most notable

accomplishment was conceiving the ideas of differential and integral calculus independently and simultaneously with Isaac Newton's similar conceptions.

- 1300 years ago, in 646, in Japan, the Nara period begins.

- 500th anniversary of Pietro Perugino's birth (1446 – 1523, aged 77, Italian painter, 6 years older than Leonardo da Vinci, but died 4 years after him).

- 400 years ago, in 1546, Michelangelo, 71, was appointed chief architect at St. Peter's Basilica in Rome, and of the Farnese Palace. The process of replacing the 1200 years old Constantinian basilica of the 4th century had been underway for fifty years, and in 1506 foundations had been laid to the plans of Bramante. Successive architects had worked on it, but little progress had been made. Michelangelo was persuaded to take over the project. He returned to the concepts of Bramante, and developed his ideas for a centrally planned church, strengthening the structure both physically and visually. The dome was not completed until after his death.

Italy, Vatican, Basilica Papale di San Pietro (1506), an ancient Egyptian obelisk (center right, of red granite, 25.5 m, 41 m total, from Heliopolis, Egypt, 2400 BC, moved by Emperor Augustus in 30 BC to Alexandria, in 37 to Rome, here in 1586).

- 300 years ago, in 1646, Jean Dedieu (or de Dieu) was born in Arles (1646 – 1727, aged 81, French sculptor). He is one of the ancestors of the author.

- Winston Churchill's "Iron Curtain" speech warns of Soviet expansion. The Cold War begins.
- The first automatic electronic digital computer, ENIAC, is dedicated at the University of Pennsylvania.
- The US Army makes radar contact with the Moon (400,000 km away) for the first time.

1947 –

- 10 February - Peace treaties for Italy, Romania, Bulgaria, Hungary, and Finland are signed in Paris.

- 11 February – 100th anniversary of the birth of Thomas Alva Edison (February 11, 1847 – October 18, 1931, aged 84.6), American inventor and businessman, who is America's greatest inventor. He developed many devices that greatly influenced life around the world, including the phonograph, the motion picture camera, and the practical electric light bulb.
- 12 March - Harry Truman establishes the Truman Doctrine of containment of Communism.

- 21 April – 2700 years ago, in 753 BC, is the founding of Rome (traditional date).

- 29 September - 400th anniversary of the birth of Miguel de Cervantes (29 Sep 1547 – 22 April 1616, aged 68.4, the greatest writer in the Spanish language, and one of the world's best novelists). His masterpiece is Don Quixote (first volume was published in 1605 (age 58), in English in 1612 (age 65), second volume in 1615 (age 68, a few months before his death), in English in 1620 (4 years after his death))),

- 500th anniversary of the birth of Luca Pacioli (Fra Luca Bartolomeo de Pacioli (c. 1447 – 1517, aged 70)), Italian mathematician, Franciscan friar, collaborator with Leonardo da Vinci, and an early contributor to the field now known as accounting. He is referred to as "The Father of Accounting and Bookkeeping", and he was the first author to publish a work on the double-entry system of book-keeping.

Invention of the first practical transistor.
Breaking of the sound barrier.

1948 –

- 18 May - 900th anniversary of the birth of Omar Khayyam (18 May 1048 – 4 December 1131, aged 83.5) Persian mathematician, astronomer, and poet.

- 2 June – 500th anniversary of Domenico Ghirlandaio's birth (2 June 1448 – 11 Jan 1494, aged 45.6, Italian painter, 3.8 years older than Leonardo da Vinci). He was a master in fresco painting, perspective, figure drawing and portraiture, and had the largest workshop in Florence.

- 10 December - 56 member states of the United Nations agreed on a catalogue of inalienable rights valid for all people. "All human beings are born free and equal in dignity and rights." This is the first sentence of the Universal Declaration of Human Rights.

Edwin Land (1909 – 1991, US) invents the Polaroid Land camera.

- 400th anniversary of the birth of Giordano Bruno (Latin: Iordanus Brunus Nolanus; 1548 – 17 February 1600, aged 51), born Filippo Bruno, Italian mathematician, Dominican friar, philosopher, poet, and cosmological theorist.

1949 –

- 4 April - twelve nations sign the North Atlantic Treaty establishing NATO.

28 August - 200th anniversary of the birth of Johann Wolfgang von Goethe (28 August 1749 – 22 March 1832, aged 82.6), German writer and statesman. His works include four novels; epic and lyric poetry; prose and verse dramas; memoirs; an autobiography; literary and aesthetic criticism; and treatises on botany, anatomy, and color.

- 2500th anniversary of the birth, in 551 BC, of Confucius, founder of Confucianism. The Confucius Temple in Qufu was built to honor Confucius—the great philosopher and educator who lived from 551 BC to 479 BC (aged 72). Also, a Confucius Museum opened in Qufu in 2018. Confucius' quotes: "Do not impose on others what you yourself do not desire." "When a country is governed well, poverty and mean condition are things to be ashamed of. When a country is governed poorly, riches and honor are things to be ashamed of."

- 500th anniversary of the birth of Lorenzo de' Medici (il Magnifico) (1 January 1449 – 8 April 1492, aged 43.3, Lord of Florence from the age of 20.9, for 22.4 years (2 Dec 1469 – 8 April 1492)).

- 100 years ago, in 1849, the safety pin was invented.

1950 –

- 15 January – 100th anniversary of the birth of Mihai Eminescu (15 January 1850 – 15 June 1889, aged 39 years and 5 months), poet, novelist and journalist, generally regarded as the most famous and influential Romanian poet.

- 5100 years ago, in 3150 BC, started the first dynasty of Egypt.

- 800 years ago, in 1150, Université de Sorbonne was founded in Paris.

Paris: Rue Soufflot (from Panthéon, looking north-west to Jardin du Luxembourg (1612, back), and Tour Eiffel (1889, 324 m)), with the Université Paris 1 Panthéon-Sorbonne (1150, 1971, right).

- 500th anniversary of the birth of Luca Signorelli (c. 1450, Cortona (80 km southeast of Florence, 160 km north of Rome, elevation 500 m) — 16 October 1523, Cortona, aged 73), Italian painter, born Luca d'Egidio di Ventura in Cortona, Tuscany (some sources call him Luca da Cortona). Luca Signorelli was 2 years older than Leonardo da Vinci, and died 4 years after him.

– 300 years ago, in 1650, Rembrandt, 44, painted Christ Appearing to Mary Magdalene, 'Noli me tangere', and a Self-Portrait.

- 100 years ago, in 1850, the Little Ice Age, for over 550 years, from around 1300, ends around this time. Several possible causes are: cyclical lows in solar radiation, heightened volcanic activity, changes in the ocean circulation, variations in Earth's orbit and axial tilt (orbital forcing), and inherent variability in global climate.

The first modern credit card Diners Club is introduced in the U.S.

Rembrandt, 44, 1650, Self-Portrait.

1951 –

- 27 February - The Twenty-second Amendment to the United States Constitution, limiting Presidents to two terms, is ratified.

- 14 June – the computer UNIVAC I is dedicated by the U.S. Census Bureau.

1952 –

– 15 April – 500th anniversary of the birth of Leonardo da Vinci (full name Leonardo di ser Piero da Vinci, 15 April 1452, Anchiano near Vinci (25 km west of Florence, on a Tuscan hill, in the lower valley of the Arno River), Republic of Florence (ruled by de Medici) – 2 May 1519, Amboise, Kingdom of France, aged 67 years and 17 days), Italian polymath whose areas of interest included invention, painting, sculpting, architecture, science, music, mathematics, engineering, literature, anatomy, geology, astronomy, optics, botany, hydrodynamics, writing, history, and cartography, but he did not publish his findings. He is the father of paleontology, ichnology, and architecture, and is one of the greatest painters of all time.

- 500 years ago, in 1452 - invention of the harpsichord (a precursor of the piano, which will be invented 250 years later, around 1700).

Chapter 2. 1953 - 1962

__1953__ –

- 20 January - Dwight David "Ike" Eisenhower, 62.3, (14 Oct 1890 – 28 March 1969, aged 78.4) was inaugurated as the 34th U.S. President (20 Jan 1953 – 20 Jan 1961, 8 years). During World War II, he was a five-star general in the United States Army, and served as Supreme Commander of the Allied Expeditionary Forces in Europe.

- 17 February – 300th anniversary of the birth of Arcangelo Corelli (17 February 1653 – 8 January 1713, aged 59.9), Italian violinist and composer.

- 5 March – Joseph Stalin died (18 Dec 1878 – 5 March 1953, aged 74.2, dictator of the Soviet Union for 29 years). On September 7 Nikita Khrushchev (1894 – 1971) takes power in the Soviet Union and starts some reforms.

- 29 May – 500 years ago, in 1453 - the Fall of Constantinople, to an Ottoman army under Sultan Mehmed II (21 years old), marks the end, after 1168 years (285 – 1453), of the Eastern Roman Empire, the death of the last Roman Emperor Constantine XI Palaiologos, and the beginning of the Classical Age of the Ottoman Empire.

- 400 years ago, in 1553, Portuguese founded a settlement at Macau, China - on the western side of the Pearl River Delta, 60 km southwest, and across, from present-day Hong Kong.

1 September - 300th anniversary of the birth of Johann Pachelbel (baptized 1 September 1653 – buried 9 March 1706, aged 52.5) German composer, organist, and teacher.

18 September - 1900th anniversary of the birth of Trajan (18 Sep 53 – 8 August 117, aged 63.9). Roman emperor for 19.6 years,

from 27 Jan 98 (age 44.3) to 8 Aug 117 AD. Officially declared by the Senate optimus princeps, Trajan is remembered as a successful soldier-emperor, who presided over the greatest military expansion in Roman history, leading the empire to attain its maximum territorial extent by the time of his death, with conquests in Dacia, Arabia, Armenia, and Mesopotamia.

1954 –

- 900 years ago, in 1054, Pope Leo IX (who ascended to the papal throne on 12 Feb 1049, for 5 years, until his death in 1054) excommunicated before his death, in 1054, Patriarch of Constantinople, Michael Cerularius (Patriarch for 16 years, 1043 – 1059, who also excommunicated Pope Leo IX), which caused the Great Schism in the Christian church, still existing today. It is also called The East-West Schism, which divided the Christian church into Western Catholicism and Eastern Orthodoxy.

- 700th anniversary of the birth of Marco Polo (1254, Venice – 8 January 1324, Venice, aged 69.5, resting place Chiesa di San Lorenzo, Sestiere di Castello, Venezia, Italian merchant, explorer (1271 (at 17) – 1295 (at 41), for 24 years, with his father and uncle), and writer: Livres des merveilles du monde (Book of the Marvels of the World) circa 1300).

Italy, Venezia - The Doge Francesco Foscari kneeling before the Winged Lion, the symbol of Venice, which holds the book quoting *"Pax Tibi Marce Evangelista Meus"* (Peace to you, Mark, my evangelist).

- 9 March – 500th anniversary of the birth of Amerigo Vespucci (9 March 1454, Republic of Florence – 22 February 1512, Seville, Spain, aged 57.9), Italian explorer, financier, navigator and cartographer. He became a naturalized citizen of the Crown of Castile at 51, in 1505. Vespucci, 48, first demonstrated, in about 1502, that Brazil and the West Indies did not represent Asia's eastern outskirts, as initially conjectured from Columbus' voyages, but instead constituted an entirely separate landmass, previously unknown to people of the Old World. This second super continent came to be termed "Americas", deriving its name from Americus, the Latin version of Vespucci's first name.

- 29 April – 100th anniversary of the birth of Jules Henri Poincaré (29 April 1854 – 17 July 1912, aged 58.2), French mathematician, theoretical physicist, engineer, and philosopher of science. He is often described as a polymath, and in mathematics as "The Last Universalist," since he excelled in all fields of the discipline as it existed during his lifetime. One of his doctorands was Dimitrie Pompeiu (4 Oct 1873 – 8 Oct 1954, aged 81years and 4 days), renowned mathematician.

Japan, Sendai, the author at the Mathematical Institute at Tohoku University (founded in 1907, the third oldest Imperial University in Japan).

1955 –

- 18 April - Albert Einstein passed away aged 76.1 (14 March 1879 – 18 April 1955). He was a German-born theoretical physicist, who developed the theory of relativity.

- 1900th anniversary of the birth of Epictetus (55 – 135, aged 80), Greek Stoic philosopher (quote: It's not what happens to you, but how you react to it, that matters.).

- 100 years ago, in 1855, Bessemer industrial process enables steel to be mass-produced.

1956 –

- 27 January – 200th anniversary of the birth of Wolfgang Amadeus Mozart (27 January 1756 – 5 December 1791, aged 35.8), a prolific and very influential Austrian composer.

- 100 years ago, in 1856, the first large petroleum refinery was built in Ploiești, Romania, using the abundant oil available in Romania.

1957 –

- 16 January - Arturo Toscanini passed away (25 March 1867 – 16 Jan 1957, aged 89.8, the greatest Italian conductor, Music Director at La Scala: 1898 – 1908 and 1921 - 1929).

- 20 March - 2000th anniversary of the birth of Publius Ovidius Naso (20 March 43 BC, Sulmo, Roman Empire (now Sulmona, Italy) – 17 AD, Tomis, Moesia, Roman Empire (now Constanța, Romania), aged circa 59), great Roman poet. Sulmo was in an Apennine valley, 120 km east of Rome, in Roman Republic (now Sulmona, in the province of L'Aquila in Abruzzo, Italy). In 8 AD, Ovidius, 50, was exiled by Augustus, 71, to Tomis, Scythia Minor, Roman Empire (now Constanța, Romania). About 9 years later he died there.

When Ovidius was born, Vergilius was 26 years 5 months and 5 days, returned to Mantova, and continued to work on the Eclogues. Horatius was 21 years, 3 months and 12 days.

Constanta, Romania, Piazza Ovidiu: Statue of Publius Ovidius Naso (20 March 43 BC, in Sulmona – 17, in Tomis, Moesia (now Constanta, Romania), aged circa 59, close to the place where Ovidius died.

- 300 years ago, in 1657, Christiaan Huygens, 28, (14 April 1629 – 8 July 1695, aged 66.2, Dutch mathematician, physicist, astronomer and inventor) developed the first functional pendulum clock, based on the learnings of Galileo Galilei, and became the most accurate timekeeper for almost 270 years, and it is still in use.

- 22 February – 100th anniversary of the birth of Heinrich Rudolf Hertz (22 February 1857 – 1 January 1894, aged 36.8), German physicist who first proved the existence of the electromagnetic waves theorized by James Clerk Maxwell's electromagnetic theory of light. The unit of frequency — cycle per second — was named the "hertz" in his honor.

- 30 November - Beniamino Gigli passed away (20 March 1890 – 30 Nov 1957, aged 67.6, great Italian opera tenor).

1958 –

- 1 January - the European Economic Community (EEC) is founded.

- 18 December - the United States launches SCORE, the world's first communications satellite.

- 400th anniversary of the birth of Michael the Brave (Mihai Viteazul; 1558 – 9 August 1601, aged 43), the Prince of Wallachia (as Michael II, 1593–1601), Prince of Moldavia (1600), and de facto ruler of Transylvania (1599–1600). He is the first to create the Romanian unity.

Romania, Bucharest: Church built by Mihai Viteazul.

1959 –

- 500th anniversary of Lorenzo di Credi's birth (1459 – 12 Jan 1537, aged 78, Italian painter, 7 years younger than Leonardo da Vinci).

10 September - 300th anniversary of the birth of Henry Purcell (c. 10 September 1659 – 21 November 1695, aged 36.2), English composer.

1960 –

- 2 May - 300th anniversary of the birth of Alessandro Scarlatti (2 May 1660 – 22 October 1725, aged 65.4) Italian Baroque composer, known especially for his operas and chamber cantatas.

He was the father of two other composers, Domenico Scarlatti and Pietro Filippo Scarlatti.

- 19 June – 2200 years ago, in 240 BC, Eratosthenes of Cyrene (now in Libya), 36, (276 BC – 194 BC, aged 82, Greek mathematician, geographer, poet, astronomer, and music theorist. He was the chief librarian at the Library of Alexandria. He invented the discipline of geography, including the terminology used today.) estimated the circumference of Earth to be nearly 250,000 stadia (40,233 km (1 stadia = 0.16 km), not far from the correct equatorial circumference 40,075 km (equatorial radius is 6,378.137 km); polar circumference is 40,007 km).

- November - 300 years ago, in 1660, The Royale Society was founded in London, England.

1961 –

- 20 January - John Fitzgerald "Jack" Kennedy, 43.7, (29 May 1917 – 22 Nov 1963, aged 46.5) was inaugurated as the 35th President of the United States, for 2.8 years, from 20 January 1961 until 22 November 1963.
- 15 September – the author started as a student at the Faculty of Mathematics.

- 300 years ago, in 1661, Rembrandt, 55, painted Lighting Study of an Old Man in Profile, The Circumcision in the Stable, The Virgin of Sorrow, Titus Posing for a Study of an Angel, St. Matthew and the Angel, The Apostle Bartholomew, The Apostle Simon, The Apostle James the Greater, The Apostle James the Less, or Christ with a Staff, Self-portrait as the Apostle Paul, Two Moors, The Small Margaretha de Geer, Portrait of Jacob Trip, Portrait of Margaretha de Geer.

Rembrandt, 55, 1661, Self-portrait as the Apostle Paul

1962 –

- 2600th anniversary of the birth of Solon, 638 BC - 558 BC, aged 80, an Athenian statesman and poet.

23 January - 100th anniversary of the birth of David Hilbert (23 Jan 1862 – 14 Feb 1943, aged 81 years and 22 days), important German mathematician.

- 10 July - Telstar 1, built by Bell Telephone Laboratories, USA, was launched on top of a Thor-Delta rocket at Cape Canaveral LC-17, Florida. It successfully relayed through space the first television pictures, telephone calls, fax images and provided the first live transatlantic television feed on 23 July.

22 August – 100th anniversary of the birth of Claude Debussy (22 August 1862 – 25 March 1918, aged 55.6, French composer).

18 November – Niels Henrik David Bohr passed away aged 77.1 (7 Oct 1885 – 18 Nov 1962). Danish physicist who made foundational contributions to understanding atomic structure and quantum theory, for which he received the Nobel Prize in Physics in 1922.

Chapter 3. 1963 - 1972

1963 –

- 8 January - After 457 years, Leonardo Da Vinci's Mona Lisa (or La Gioconda) from Louvre was exhibited in the United States for the first time, at the National Gallery of Art in Washington, D.C.

U. S. A., Washington, D.C. (1790) in 2007, National Gallery of Art (1937, in the National Mall).

- 29 January - Robert Frost passed away (26 March 1874, San Francisco, CA – 29 Jan 1963, Boston, MA, aged 88.8). He was an American poet influenced by Horatius' "Ars Poetica", initially published in England, before it was published in America. Known for his realistic depictions of rural life, and his command of American colloquial speech, Frost frequently wrote about settings from rural life in New England, around Boston.

– 24 February – 500th anniversary of Pico della Mirandola's birth (24 February 1463, Mirandola (110 km southwest of Venezia), Duchy of Mirandola – 17 November 1494, Firenze, aged 31.7), Italian nobleman and philosopher.

- 16 June – 650th anniversary of the birth of Giovanni Boccaccio (16 June 1313 – 21 December 1375, aged 62.5, Italian writer, poet, correspondent of Petrarca (who was almost 9 years older than Boccaccio), and an important Renaissance humanist.

- 17 October - Jacques Hadamard passed away (8 Dec 1865 – 17 Oct 1963, aged 97.8), French mathematician who made major contributions in number theory, complex function theory, differential geometry and partial differential equations.

- 22 November – U. S. President John F. Kennedy died of gun wounds, aged 46.5 years.
Lyndon Baines Johnson, 55.2, (27 Aug 1908- 22 Jan 1973, aged 65.4) was inaugurated as the 36th President of the United States, for 5.1 years, from 22 Nov 1963 to 20 Jan 1969. Formerly he was the 37th Vice President of the United States, serving with President John F. Kennedy.

- 300 years ago, in 1663, Robert Hooke, 28, (28 July 1635 – 3 March 1703, aged 67.6) discovered cells using a microscope.

- 100 years ago, in 1863 - Formation of the International Red Cross, which was followed by the adoption of the First Geneva Convention in 1864. Also, the first section of the London Underground opens.

1964 –

- 15 February - 400th anniversary of the birth of Galileo Galilei (15 February 1564 – 8 January 1642, aged 77.9), Italian polymath. Known for his work as mathematician, astronomer, physicist, engineer, and philosopher, Galileo has been called the "father of observational astronomy", the "father of modern physics", the "father of the scientific method", and the "father of science".

- 23 April - 400th anniversary of the birth of William Shakespeare (23 April 1564 (baptized on 26 – the only recorded date)—23 April 1616, aged 52, English poet, playwright and actor, widely regarded as the greatest writer in the English language). He was born in Stratford-upon-Avon (130 km northwest of London, and 35 km southeast of Birmingham), Warwickshire, England.

Shakespeare's quote: Love all, trust a few, do wrong to none.

- 1 May - at 4:00 AM, John George Kemeny (1926 – 1992, mathematician, President of Dartmouth College (1769, Hanover (on the Connecticut River, 180 km northwest of Boston), New Hampshire, USA, Latin: Collegium Dartmuthensis, motto: Vox clamantis in deserto (The voice of one crying out in the wilderness))), and Thomas Eugene Kurtz (1928, mathematician, Professor at Dartmouth College), ran the first computer program written in BASIC (Beginners' All-purpose Symbolic Instruction Code), an easy to learn high level programming language which they created. BASIC was eventually included on many computers.

- 300 years ago, in 1664, British troops capture New Amsterdam, after 39 years of existence, and renamed it New York.

1965 –

- 2500th anniversary of the birth of Heraclitus of Ephesus (c 535 BC – c 475 BC, aged c 60), Greek philosopher who said "The only constant is change."

- 24 January - Sir Winston Leonard Spencer-Churchill passed away (30 Nov 1874 – 24 Jan 1965, aged 90.1), British politician, statesman, army officer, and writer, who was Prime Minister of the United Kingdom from 1940 to 1945 and again from 1951 to 1955. As Prime Minister, Churchill led Britain to victory in the Second World War. Churchill's quote: It`s not enough that we do our best; sometimes we have to do what`s required.

- 15 June – 750 years ago, in 1215, King John of England signed Magna Carta Libertatum (drafted by the Archbishop of Canterbury), at Runnymede, near Windsor, 32 km west of London.

- 21 August – 550 years ago, in 1415, Prince Henrique of Portugal leads the conquest of Ceuta from the Moors, marking the beginning of the Portuguese Empire in Africa (for over 530 years).

- 28 December - 900 years ago, in 1065, St Peter's Abbey (Westminster Abbey) in London was consecrated. Between 1042 and 1052, King Edward the Confessor began rebuilding St Peter's Abbey (Westminster Abbey), to provide himself with a royal burial church. It was the first church in England built in the Romanesque style. The building was completed around 1060, and was consecrated on 28 December 1065, only a week before Edward's death on 5 January 1066. A week later, he was buried in the church; and, nine years later, his wife Edith was buried alongside him. His successor, Harold II, was probably crowned in the abbey, in 1066, although the first documented coronation is that of William the Conqueror later the same year.

The west façade and entrance of Westminster Abbey (960, 1517, Collegiate Church of St Peter at Westminster, Anglican abbey with daily services and coronations since 1066, tower height 69 m).

700th anniversary of the birth of Durante degli Alighieri (commonly known as Dante Alighieri or simply Dante; c. 1265, Republic of Florence – 1321, Ravenna, Papal States, aged 56, a major Italian poet. His Divine Comedy, originally called Comedìa (1308 – 1320, modern Italian: Commedia), and about 30 years later named Divina by Giovanni Boccaccio (16 June 1313 – 21 December 1375, aged 62.5; he was 8 years old when Dante died), is considered one of the most important poems, and one of the greatest literary work).

100 years ago, in 1865, the London Mathematical Society was founded.

Italy, June 1978, Verona (300 BC, municipium in 49 BC, elevation 59 m, population 269,000, area 206 km², on the river Adige, three of Shakespeare's (1564-1616) plays are set here), Piazza dei Signori, looking northwest to the statue of Dante Alighieri (1265 – 1321, poet (Divina Commedia (1308-1320), the Father of the Italian language, and one of the greatest poets of world literature), statesman, language theorist), Loggia del Consiglio (back).

- 550th anniversary of the birth of Piero della Francesca (c. 1415–1492, aged 77) Italian painter and mathematician.

- 400 years ago, in 1565 - Invention of the graphite pencil (in a wooden holder) by Conrad Gesner. Modernized in 1812.

<u>1966</u> –

- 10 May – The young author and his wife, after receiving their Master's of Science degrees in Mathematics.

May 10, 1966: M. and S. Dediu, both with MS in Mathematics.

- 2500 years ago, in 534 BC, theatre was born in Athens. A priest of Dionysus (a god of fertility and wine in Greece), by the name of Thespis, engages in a dialogue with the chorus, becoming the first actor. Thespis is also the first winner of a theatrical award. He takes the prize in the first competition for tragedy, held in Athens in 534 BC.

1967 –

- 850 years ago, in 1117, the University of Oxford (Motto: Dominus illuminatio mea) is founded. It is the oldest university in the United Kingdom.

- 700th anniversary of the birth of Giotto di Bondone (c. 1267 – January 8, 1337, aged 69.5, known as Giotto, Italian painter and architect from Florence). Giotto painted a portrait of Dante, who was two years older. In Florence there is also Il Campanile di Giotto, started on 19 July 1334, when Giotto was 67.

- 13 February - American scientists discovered on this day, in the National Library of Spain, the 477 years old sketch of the design for an adding machine, from 1490, by Leonardo da Vinci, 38.

- 30 March – 100 years ago, in 1867, The United States purchases Alaska (1.5 M km^2 for \$7.2 M (\$4.8/ km^2), equivalent to about \$105 M in 2016) from Russia.

- 15 May - 400th anniversary of the birth of Claudio Monteverdi (15 May 1567 – 29 Nov 1643, aged 76.5, great Italian composer).

Trieste - 23 Oct 2009, inside Teatro Verdi, commemoration dedicated to Claudio Monteverdi (1567-1643, composer, gambist, singer, and Catholic priest). He wrote 9 books of Madrigali (1587-1643, the ninth book was published posthumously in 1651), 18 operas, but only L'Orfeo (1609), Il ritorno d'Ulisse in patria (1640), L'incoronazione di Poppea (1642), and the famous aria, Lamento, from his second opera L'Arianna (1608), have survived, and sacred music (Vespro della Beata Vergine (1610), Messa in illo tempore (1610), Mass of Thanksgiving (1631), Messa a 4 da Cappela(1641), and others). Monteverdi developed two styles of composition – the heritage of Renaissance polyphony and the new basso continuo technique of the Baroque. He wrote one of the earliest operas, *L'Orfeo that* is the earliest surviving opera still regularly performed.

100 years ago, in 1867, Claude Monet, 27, finished the paintings Saint Germain l'Auxerrois and Women in the Garden.

Claude Monet, 27, 1867, Saint Germain l'Auxerrois

Women in the Garden by Claude Monet, 27, 1867

1968 –

- 2400 years ago, in 432 BC, the building of the Parthenon in Athens was completed, after 15 years of work (classical temple in Athens, Greece, 447 BC – 432 BC, height 13.72 m, 69.5 m by 30.9 m)

Chicago (1833): above entrance decorations of the Tribune Tower (1925, 36 floors, 141 m, for Chicago Tribune (1847)), with stones from famous places around the world, and from the Moon, including Harvard University, Arc de Triomph, Switzerland, Great Wall, Parthenon, Taj Mahal, Notre-Dame, and St. Peter's Basilica.

- 450th anniversary of the birth of Tintoretto (1518 – 1594, aged 76) noted Italian (Venetian) painter.

- 400 years ago, in 1568, The Transylvanian Diet, under the patronage of the prince John Sigismund Zápolya, the king of Hungary as John II, inspired by the teachings of Ferenc Dávid, the founder of the Unitarian Church of Transylvania, promulgated the Edict of Torda, the first law of freedom of religion and of conscience in the World.

- 5 January - in Czechoslovakia, the Communist Party's Central Committee votes out Antonin Novotny, 64, (1904 – 1975, aged 71) as First Secretary, and replaces him with Alexander Dubcek, 47, (1921 – 1992, aged 71). Novotny remains the country's president, but it is the beginning of what will be known as the Prague Spring – a reference to the blossoming of reforms called "socialism with a human face", until the Soviet invasion.

- 30 September - the first Boeing 747 rolled out of its custom-built assembly plant in Everett, Washington State, USA. From the beginning, everything about the plane, which will be known as the queen of the skies, was big. After 50 years, in 2018, the plane is still very good.

- 3 November – The author's family in a small park.

3 November 1968. From left: Sofia (mother, teacher of mathematics), Ovidiu (son, two years birthday), Horațiu (son, 8 months) and M. Dediu (father, researcher at the Institute of Mathematics).

Solzhenitsyn, 50, completes his masterwork, "The Gulag Archipelago", a history of the labor camps in which he served. The book would become a powerful indictment of the Soviet dictator Joseph Stalin, who used the camps to hold political prisoners, in an attempt to destroy the opposition to the Soviet totalitarian state.

1969 –

- 20 January - Richard Milhous Nixon, 56, (9 Jan 1913 – 22 April 1994, aged 81.3) was the 37th President of the United States, for 5.6 years, from 20 Jan 1969 until 9 Aug 1974, when he resigned the office. He had previously served as the 36th Vice President of the United States, with President Dwight Eisenhower, from 1953 to 1961, and prior to that as both a U.S. Representative and Senator from California.

- 3 May – 500th anniversary of the birth of Niccolò di Bernardo dei Machiavelli (3 May 1469 – 21 June 1527, aged 58.1), Italian diplomat, politician, historian, philosopher, humanist, writer, playwright and poet.

- 450 years ago, in 1519 – beginning of the Spanish expedition commanded by the Portuguese explorer Ferdinand Magellan (3 Feb 1480, Portugal – 27 April 1521, Philippines, aged 41.2), and, after the death of Magellan, finished by Elcano, which was the first to circumnavigate the Earth, after 3 years, in 1522, returning with only 18 men out of the original 237.

- 20 July, 9:56 PM Boston time (21 July, 2:56 UTC) – Neil Armstrong, 38.9, (5 Aug 1930 – 25 Aug 2012, aged 82 years and 20 days) set his left boot on the lunar surface.

1 Dec 2007, Washington, D.C. (1790): the author (64) near the Lunar Module Eagle from Apollo 11 (1969), at the National Air and Space Museum (1976).

– 4 August – 50 years ago, in 1919, Musée Rodin opens to the public, and holds over 6,000 sculptures, 7,000 of his drawings and prints, in chalk and charcoal, and thirteen drypoints. He also produced a single lithograph. The Musée Rodin is in the former Hôtel Biron (1727 – 1732, 77 Rue de Varenne, 240 m east of Tombeau de Napoléon Ier in Les Invalides).

- 15 August: 200th anniversary of the birth of Napoleone di Buonaparte (15 Aug 1769, Corsica, France – 5 May 1821, Longwood House, Saint Helena Island, England, aged 51.7, after being, as Napoléon, Emperor of the French for 9.9 years, King of Italy for 9 years, Protector of the Confederation of the Rhine (Germany) for 7.2 years, First Consul of France for 4.5 years).

- 25 August – Just 36 days after the author's family watched on TV in direct live Neil Armstrong, 38.9, setting his left boot on the lunar surface, they relax near the Black Sea.

August 25, 1969, in a park near the Black Sea: M. and S. Dediu with sons Horațiu and Ovidiu, very happy that a man was on the Moon.

- 14 September - 200th anniversary of the birth of Alexander von Humboldt (14 Sep 1769 – 6 May 1859, aged 89.6, German naturalist).

Église du Dôme (1708, 107 m height, inspired by St. Peter's Basilica in Rome,1626) in the center of L'Hôtel National des Invalides (1678, by Louis XIV, in the 7th arrondissement, with military museums and monuments and the burial site for Napoleon Bonaparte (1769-1821)). Napoleon was entombed under the Dôme of the Invalides, in a tomb made of red quartzite and resting on a green granite base, which was finished in 1861.

1970 –

- 21 February – The author (researcher and doctorand) with his wife (teacher) in a short vacation in the mountains full of snow.

21 February 1970 – Bucegi Mountains between Gârbova and Clăbucet

- 9 November - Charles de Gaulle passed away (22 Nov 1890 – 9 Nov 1970, aged 79.9, 13 days before 80), French army officer and statesman who led the French Resistance against Nazi Germany in World War II and was President of France for 10.2 years.

17 December – 200th anniversary of the birth of Ludwig van Beethoven (baptized 17 December 1770 – 26 March 1827, aged 56.2), great German composer and pianist.

Paris - The central part of the façade of L'Opéra de Paris (1875): composers Daniel Auber (1782–1871, left), Ludwig van Beethoven (1770–1827, second), Wolfgang Amadeus Mozart (1756–1791, center) and Gaspare Spontini (1774–1851, right).

- 1150 years ago, in 820, Algebrae et Alumcabola Algorithm was published by Algoritmi, 40, (circa 780 – c 850, in Baghdad, aged c 70, Persian scholar who produced works in mathematics (founder of parts of algebra and algorithm), geography and astronomy).

- 550 years ago, in 1420, the construction of the Chinese Forbidden City was completed in Beijing – imperial palace for 492 years, from 1420 to 1912.

- 450th anniversary of the birth of Andrea Amati (c. 1520 – c. 1578, aged 58), the earliest maker of violins, whose instruments still survive today.

- 350 years ago, in 1620, The Brownist Pilgrims from England arrived in the ship Mayflower at Cape Cod in America.

- 300 years ago, in 1670, Bartolomé Esteban Murillo, 53, (31 Dec 1617 – 3 April 1682, aged 64.2, Spanish painter), painted "A Girl and Her Duenna", now at the National Gallery of Art in Washington, D.C.

A Girl and Her Duenna by Bartolomé Esteban Murillo, 53, 1670, (31 Dec 1617 – 3 April 1682, aged 64.2, Spanish painter), now at the National Gallery of Art in Washington, D.C.

1971 –

- 1650 years ago, in 321, Roman Emperor Constantine the Great (27 Feb 272 – 22 May 337, aged 65.2, Emperor for 30.8 years: 25 July 306 – 22 May 337) makes the day of the Sun God Sol Invictus (Sunday) a holy day, and a day of rest for Christians.

- 1550 years ago, in 421, according to legend, the city of Venezia (Venice) was founded by Romans fleeing from Germans.

Italia, Venezia: the west and south facades of Palazzo Ducale (circa 820 – 1420), and the street Riva degli Schiavoni (right).

- 400th anniversary of the birth of Johannes Kepler (1571 – 1630, aged 59), German mathematician, astronomer and philosopher.

- 8 June - 300th anniversary of the birth of Tomaso Albinoni (8 June 1671, in Venezia – 17 January 1751, aged 79.5). He was an older contemporaneous Italian composer with Vivaldi and Bach (Albinoni was born 6.7 years before Vivaldi, and 13.8 years before

Bach, then Albinoni died 9.5 years after Vivaldi, and almost half a year after Bach).

- 30 August – 100th anniversary of the birth of Ernest Rutherford (30 August 1871 – 19 October 1937, aged 66.1), a New Zealand-born British physicist, who came to be known as the father of nuclear physics.

1972 –

- 15 January - 350th anniversary of the birth of Molière (15 Jan 1622 – 17 Feb 1673, aged 51.1, full name Jean-Baptiste Poquelin, known by his stage name Molière, a French playwright, actor and poet).

- October - the First International Conference on Computer Communications is held in Washington, D.C., and hosts the first public demonstration of ARPAnet, a precursor of the Internet.

- 27 December – 150th anniversary of the birth of Louis Pasteur (December 27, 1822 – September 28, 1895, aged 72.7), French biologist, microbiologist and chemist, renowned for his discoveries of the principles of vaccination, microbial fermentation, and pasteurization. He is remembered for his remarkable breakthroughs in the causes and prevention of diseases, and his discoveries have saved many lives ever since.

Chapter 4. 1973 - 1982

1973 –

- 2800 years ago started the reign of King Xuan (827 BC – 782 BC, 45 years) of the Western Zhou Dynasty in China.

- 19 February – 500th anniversary of the birth of Nicolaus Copernicus (19 February 1473 – 24 May 1543, aged 70.2), a mathematician, astronomer and economist, who formulated a model of the universe that placed the Sun, rather than the Earth, at the center of the universe, independently of Aristarchus of Samos (310 BC – 230 BC), who had formulated such a model some 1780 years earlier. The publication of Copernicus' model in his book De revolutionibus orbium coelestium (On the Revolutions of the Celestial Spheres), just before his death in 1543, was a major event in the history of science.

- 7 May - 2400th anniversary of the birth of Plato (7 May 427 BC – 347 BC, aged 80), great Greek philosopher, student of Socrates (43 years older than Plato), teacher of Aristotle (43 years younger than Plato), the founder of the Academy in Athens, the first institution of higher learning in the world. Plato's quotes: "Access to power must be confined to those who are not in love with it." "Any man may easily do harm, but not every man can do good to another." "Excess generally causes reaction, and produces a change in the opposite direction, whether it be in the seasons, or in individuals, or in governments."

- 19 June - 350th anniversary of the birth of Blaise Pascal (19 June 1623 – 19 August 1662, aged 39 years and 2 months), important French mathematician, physicist, inventor, and writer. He was a child prodigy, who was educated by his father.

- 29 September - W. H. Auden passes away (21 Feb 1907 in York, UK – 29 Sep 1973 in Vienna, Austria, aged 66.6). He was an English-American poet influenced by Horatius' "Ars Poetica", who distinguished himself for his stylistic and technical achievement.

- 300 years ago, in 1673, Antonie van Leeuwenhoek, 41, (24 Oct 1632 – 26 August 1723, aged 90.8, Dutch microbiologist) was the first to observe microbes with a homemade microscope.

1974 –

- 22 April – - 250th anniversary of the birth of Immanuel Kant (22 April 1724 – 12 February 1804, aged 79.8), German philosopher who is a central figure in modern philosophy.

- 25 April - 100th anniversary of the birth of Guglielmo Marconi (25 April 1874 – 20 July 1937, aged 63.2), Italian inventor and electrical engineer, known for his pioneering work on long-distance radio transmission, and for his development of Marconi's law and a radio telegraph system. He is the inventor of radio, and he shared the 1909 Nobel Prize in Physics with Karl Ferdinand Braun "in recognition of their contributions to the development of wireless telegraphy". Marconi was also an entrepreneur, businessman, and founder of The Wireless Telegraph & Signal Company in the United Kingdom in 1897 (which became the Marconi Company). In 1931, he, 57, set up the Vatican Radio for Pope Pius XI.

- April - the world population reaches 4 billions of people, estimated by the United States Census Bureau.

- 9 August - Gerald Rudolph Ford Jr., 61, (14 July 1913 – 26 Dec 2006, aged 93.4) was inaugurated as the 38th President of the United States, for 2.4 years, from 9 August 1974 to 20 January 1977. Before he served as the 40th Vice President of the United States, with President Richard Nixon, from December 1973 to 9 August 1974.

- 100 years ago, in 1874, Claude Monet, 34, painted The Boats Regatta at Argenteuil.

Claude Monet, 34, 1874, The Boats Regatta at Argenteuil

1975 –

- 2300th anniversary of the birth of Euclid (325 BC – 265 BC, aged 60). Great Greek mathematician, the father of geometry. He arrived with his parents in Alexandria in 322 BC, when he was 3 years old, about ten years after its founding, in 332 BC, by Alexander the Great, 24, (356 BC – 323 BC, aged 32.8). It is probable that he attended Plato's Academy in Athens, and received his mathematical training from students of Plato. He was active in Alexandria during the reign of Ptolemy I (323 BC–283 BC, 40 years). Alexandria was then the largest city in the western world, and the center of both the papyrus industry, and the book trade. Ptolemy had created the great library at Alexandria, which was known as the Museum, because it was considered a house of the muses for the arts and sciences. Many scholars worked and taught there, and that is where Euclid wrote The Elements. His 13 books Elements, based on the works of Thales, Pythagoras, Plato, Eudoxus, Aristotle, Menaechmus and others, are the most influential books in the history of mathematics, the most famous, and most published mathematical work in history. serving as the main textbook for teaching mathematics (especially geometry) from the time of its publication (around 280 BC, when he was 45 years old) for more than 2200 years. In the Elements, Euclid deduced the principles of what is now called Euclidean geometry from a small set of axioms. He began with accepted mathematical truths, axioms and postulates, and demonstrated logically 467 propositions in plane and solid geometry. One of the proofs was for the theorem of Pythagoras, proving that the equation is always true for every right triangle. The Elements was the most widely used textbook of all time, has appeared in more than 1,000 editions since printing was invented, was still found in classrooms until about 50 years ago, and have sold more copies than any book other than the Bible. He introduced a system of rigorous mathematical proofs that remains the basis of mathematics to this day. Euclid also wrote works on perspective, conic sections, spherical geometry, number theory, and rigor Euclid is the anglicized version of the Greek name, which means "renowned, glorious". Campanus translated The Elements from Arabic to Latin, and the first printed edition appeared in Venice in 1482. The first English translation of The Elements was by the mathematician John Dee in 1570. Dee's lectures and writings revived interest in mathematics in England. His translation was from a Latin translation of an Arabic translation of the original Greek.

- 2000 years ago, in 25 BC, Pantheon was completed by Agrippa (38) in Roma – it is still an open church and museum.

- 950 years ago, in 1025, the Canon of Medicine by Avicenna (22 August 980, in Samanid Empire (now Uzbekistan) – 21 June 1037, in Kakuyid Emirate (now Iran), aged 56.8, Persian polymath who is regarded as one of the most significant physicians, astronomers, thinkers and writers of that period) set the standard medical textbook for over 700 years, through 18th century, in Europe. After 948 years, in 1973, Avicenna's Canon of Medicine was reprinted in New York.

- 800th anniversary of the birth of Leonardo Bonacci (or Leonardo di Pisa), nicknamed in 1838 Fibonacci (circa 1175- c. 1250, aged c. 75, filius Bonacci, Italian mathematician from the Republic of Pisa). In 1202, Fibonacci, 27, published his book Liber Abaci (Book of Calculation - historic book on arithmetic, using Hindu-Arabic numeral system, which is used today).

6 April 1978, Pisa, Cattedrale di Pisa (1092, striped-marble, left), Torre di Pisa (August 1173-1372, 55.86 m on the low side, 56.67 m on the high side, white-marble, 296 steps, right).

- 550 years ago, in 1425, The Catholic University of Leuven (Belgium) was founded by Pope Martin V.

Belgium, 19 March 1978, Bruxelles (990, population 1.1 M), from Grand Place looking to the northwest façade of a classical building.

- 6 March – 500th anniversary of the birth of Michelangelo di Lodovico Buonarroti Simoni or Michelangelo (6 March 1475, Caprese (20 km northeast of Arezzo, 40 km north of Cortona, 60 km southeast of Florence) – 18 February 1564, aged 88.9 (just 16 days before 89)), great Italian sculptor, painter, and architect.

- 450th anniversary of the birth of Giovanni Pierluigi da Palestrina (1525 – 1594, aged 69) influential Italian (from Roma) composer of sacred music.

- 450 years ago, in 1525 - introduction of the modern square root symbol ($\sqrt{}$).

- 350 years ago, in 1625, New Amsterdam was founded in Manhattan, 39 years before New York, by the Dutch West India Company in North America.

- 300 years ago, in 1675, Greenwich Observatory was founded west of London.

Looking northwest to the southeast side of the South Building (1899, Astronomy Center) of Royal Observatory Greenwich (1676).

7 March – 100th anniversary of the birth of Joseph Maurice Ravel (7 March 1875 – 28 December 1937, aged 62.7), French composer, pianist and conductor. His elder contemporary was Claude Debussy. In the 1920s and 1930s Ravel was internationally regarded as France's greatest living composer.

L'Opéra de Paris was opened.

- 1 August - the Helsinki Accords, Helsinki Final Act, or Helsinki Declaration was the first act of the Conference on Security and Co-operation in Europe held in Finlandia Hall of Helsinki, Finland, during July and August 1, 1975. Thirty-five states, including the USA, UK, Canada, and most European states except Albania, signed the declaration in an attempt to improve relations between the Communist bloc and the West. The Helsinki Accords, however, were not binding, as they did not have treaty status, but they had a positive impact for the people looking for freedom in the Communist bloc.

The east side of l'Opéra de Paris (or l'Opéra Garnier, 1875), a 1,979-seat opera house, seen from Rue Halévy and Rue Glück.

1976 –

- 2600th anniversary of the birth of the first mathematician and philosopher - Thales of Miletus (ca. 624 BC – 547 BC, aged 77), 54 years older than Pythagoras, and Thales died when Pythagoras was 23. Thales' theorem, which states that if A, B and C are points on a circle, where the line AC is a diameter of the circle, then the angle ABC is a right angle.

- January - the Cray-1, the first commercially developed supercomputer, is released by Seymour Cray's (1925 – 1996, aged 71) mathematician and electrical engineer) Cray Research.

- 17 September – 150th anniversary of the birth of Georg Friedrich Bernhard Riemann (17 September 1826 – 20 July 1866, aged 39.8), great German mathematician, who made important contributions to analysis, number theory, and differential geometry.

- 4 July - 200 years ago, in 1776, The United States Declaration of Independence was adopted by the Continental Congress in Philadelphia.

Boston, USA - 11 July 2009, the author (65.6) at the northwest end of Boston Fish Pier, northwest of the Exchange Conference Center (right) a Lexington Minutemen (armed volunteers ready to go in a minute) unit in 1776 uniforms.

- 350 years ago, in 1626, St. Peter's Basilica in Vatican was completed

- 300 years ago, in 1676 - the first measurement of the speed of light: almost 300,000 km/s.

- 100 years ago, in 1876, Pierre-Auguste Renoir, known as Auguste Renoir, 35, (25 February 1841 – 3 December 1919, aged 78.8, French painter) painted Girl with Sheaf of Corn.

Girl with Sheaf of Corn by Auguste Renoir, 35, 1876, (25 February 1841 – 3 December 1919, aged 78.8, French painter).

1977 –

- 20 January - James Earl Carter Jr., 52.3, (born 1 Oct 1924, age at the end of 2018, 94.2) was inaugurated as the 39th President of the United States, for 4 years, from 20 Jan 1977 to 20 Jan 1981. He previously served as a Georgia State Senator from 1963 to 1967, and as the 76th Governor of Georgia from 1971 to 1975.

- 600th anniversary of the birth of Filippo Brunelleschi (1377 – April 15, 1446, aged 68), Italian designer and great architect, also the first modern engineer, planner and sole construction supervisor. He was one of the founding fathers of the Renaissance. He is well known for developing a technique for linear perspective in art, and for building the largest brick dome in the world – the dome of the Florence Cathedral Santa Maria del Fiore.

- 30 April – 200th anniversary of the birth of Johann Carl Friedrich Gauss (30 April 1777 – 23 February 1855, aged 77 years 9 months and 23 days, of a heart attack, in Göttingen, Kingdom of Hanover (now Lower Saxony, Germany)), German mathematician and physicist who made significant contributions to many fields, including algebra, analysis, astronomy, differential geometry, electrostatics, geodesy, geophysics, magnetic fields, matrix theory, mechanics, number theory, optics and statistics. Referred to as the Princeps mathematicorum (Latin for "the foremost of mathematicians") and "the greatest mathematician since antiquity", Gauss had an exceptional influence in many fields of mathematics and science, and is ranked among history's most influential mathematicians.

USA, the author at the University of California, Berkeley (1868), Mathematical Sciences Research Institute (1982), at 17 Gauss Way, on the hill.

28 June - 400th anniversary of the birth of Sir Peter Paul Rubens (28 June 1577 – 30 May 1640, aged 62.9, great Flemish painter, father of eight children (3 with his first wife Isabella, and 5 with his second wife Helena)).

5 September - Voyager 1 was launched in the U.S. to Jupiter and Saturn, and 35 years after leaving Earth, in 2012, was close to the boundary that separates the Solar System and interstellar space. The Solar System is enveloped in a big plasma bubble. This hot and turbulent region is created by a stream of charged particles from the Sun. Outside the plasma bubble is the space between stars in the Milky Way. Together with Voyager 2, which was launched two weeks earlier, they are the longest operating spacecraft in history and the most distant, in different directions. In 2012 Voyager 1 was more than 27 billions km from the Sun, and Voyager 2 more than 22 billions km from the Sun. The spacecrafts have enough fuel to last until around 2020. By that time, probably they will already be moving between the stars of the Milky Way.

1978 –

- 11 February - Spiaggia (Beach) di Mondello

Italy, 11 Feb 1978, the author (34.2, invited at the University of Palermo) is looking north to Spiaggia (Beach) di Mondello and Tyrrhenian Sea, 10 km northwest of Palermo, Sicilia.

- 4 March - 300th anniversary of the birth of Antonio Vivaldi (4 March 1678 – 28 July 1741, aged 63.3), great Italian (from Venezia) composer, virtuoso violinist, and teacher.

- 24 April – Mathematical Conference at Oberwolfach, Germany.

Germany (southwest), 24 April 1978, Oberwolfach (the district of Ortenau in Baden-Württemberg, elevation 323 m (270 m to 948 m), 465 km southwest of Brunswick, and 375 km southwest of Göttingen, in the central Schwarzwald (Black Forest) on the river Wolf, a tributary of the Kinzig.): Academician Prof. Dr. Gheorghe Vranceanu (77.8, right) and Dr. Michael M. Dediu (34.4) at the entrance to the Mathematisches Forschungsinstitut Oberwolfach (Mathematical Research Institute of Oberwolfach, founded in 1944 by the German mathematician Wilhelm Süss (1895-1958)).

- 1 June – The author (34.6), with his sons Ovidiu (back, 11.6) and Horatiu (10.3, right), are in Cortona, Italia, being invited at a mathematical conference.

Italy, 1 June 1978, Cortona, on the road to Il Palazzone, Villa Principesca Sec XVI, looking west to Camucia and Vale di Chiana.

- 13 July – 100 years ago, in 1878, following the Russo (with Romania, Bulgaria, Serbia and Montenegro) - Turkish War (1877 – 1878), the Treaty of Berlin (13 July 1878) recognizes formal independence of the Principality of Serbia, Montenegro, and Romania. Bulgaria becomes autonomous.

- 9 September – 150th anniversary of the birth of Count Lyov (also Lev) Nikolayevich Tolstoy (9 September 1828 – 20 November 1910, aged 82.2), sometimes referred to as Leo Tolstoy, was a Russian writer, who is regarded as one of the greatest authors of all time. He had 13 children with his wife Sophia. One of the children, Alexandra Lvovna Tolstaya, died at 95.2 in 1979.

- September – The author met Ambassador Arciniegas and his family in Rome, Italy – he was an outstanding personality, distinguished intellectual, who made remarkable contributions to the progress of our culture and civilization. He gave us a real luculliano dinner (luculliano means "most generous", or "luxurious and lavish" in reference to a meal, and comes from Lucius Licinius Lucullus (118 BC – 56 BC, (62) a Roman politician in the late Roman Republic (connected with Lucius Cornelius Sulla (139 BC – 78 BC (61))), known for his sumptuous banquets).

11 Sept 1977, Roma, Lido dei Pini di Ardea (43 km south of Rome), second from left Germán Arciniegas, 77, (1900-1999, Colombian professor, historian, author and Ambassador to the Holy See), his daughter Gabriela (left), the author (center) and his wife (right).

- 100 years ago, in 1878, the first commercial telephone exchange took place in New Haven, Connecticut.

- 50 years ago, in 1928 - discovery of penicillin by Alexander Fleming.

Also, the Kellogg-Briand Pact (not to use war to resolve disputes) was signed in Paris.by France and the United States, then by a total of 63 states, and remains in effect.

1979 –

- 2200 years ago, in 221 BC, Qin Shi Huang unified China, ended of Warring States period; this is marking the beginning of Imperial rule in China, which lasts for 2133 years, until 1912.
Construction of the Great Wall by the Qin Dynasty begins.

14 April – 350th anniversary of the birth of Christaan Huygens (14 April 1629 – 8 July 1695, aged 66.2, founder of mathematical physics, contributions in optics and mechanics, discovered Saturn's moon Titan, invention of the Huygenian eyepiece for the telescope, and invented the pendulum clock in 1656, which was a breakthrough in timekeeping, and became the most accurate timekeeper for almost 300 years)

- 27 April - Acad. Professor Gheorghe Vrănceanu, passed away in Bucharest (30 June 1900 – 27 April 1979, aged 78 years 9 months and 28 days (2 months and 3 days before his 79th birthday)). His mathematical research and results influenced many mathematicians, including T. Y. Thomas, V. V. Wagner, K. Yano, M. Dediu, A. G. Walker, K. Nomizu, S. Kobayashi.

- May - the author was invited at the University of Arizona.

USA, Arizona, Tucson (1877, elevation 728 m, population 530,000), May 1979, (the author, 35.5, was invited at the University of Arizona (1885, academic staff 3,000, students 43,000)).

- 9 August – Cleveland, USA, The Fountain of Eternal Life.

USA, Cleveland, 9 August 1979, The Fountain of Eternal Life, in front of the old Cleveland Board of Education building (1931-2013 (82 years), the author worked here in 1980-1985; from 2016 in this transformed building is Drury Plaza Hotel).

- 24 August – 1900 years ago, in 79, Mount Vesuvius erupted, burying the cities of Pompeii, Herculaneum and Stabiae in volcanic ash.

Italy, ruins of Pompeii (650 BC, in 79 covered by ash), the northwest part of Theatrum Odeon (80 BC, for music and poetry).

- 300 years ago, in 1679, the binary system, now used in all computers, was developed by Gottfried Wilhelm Leibniz, 33 years old.

- 150 years ago, in 1829, the first electric motor was built.

- 50 years ago, in 1929, Vatican City, under Pope Pius XI, is recognized as a sovereign state.

Rome (753 BC), Vatican (1929): Piazza di San Pietro (1656 – 1667, Bernini), with Moderno's façade (115 m wide, 46 m high) of the Basilica di San Pietro (1506 – 1626), and an Egyptian obelisk (1250 BC, 25.5 m, total height 40 m), moved here in 1586.

__1980__ –

- 2600th anniversary of the birth of Aesop, 620 BC – 560 BC, aged 60, ancient Greek fabulist.

- 2550th anniversary of the birth of Pythagoras (570 BC – 495 BC, aged 75), great Greek mathematician. Pythagoras of Samos was born on the Samos Island, which is a Greek island in the eastern Aegean Sea, just 1.6 km from the coast of Asia Minor, where is Turkey, about 250 km East of Athens, and 350 km North-East of Crete. Pythagoras married Theano, and they had four children: Damo, Myia, Telauges and Arignote. Pythagoras' mother was Pythais, and father Mnesarchus, a merchant who came from Tyre. Pythagoras died in Metapontum, which was an important ancient Greek city of Magna Graecia, currently in the Southern Italy, on the gulf of Tarentum, about 140 km east of Napoli (Naples), and 160 km northeast of Messina, Sicilia (Sicily). Pythagoras' theorem:

In any right triangle, the area of the square on the hypotenuse (opposite the right angle) is equal to the sum of the areas of the squares on the other two sides of the triangle.

Pythagoras' quote: "Were it not for number and its nature, nothing that exists would be clear to anybody, either in itself, or in its relation to other things...You can observe the power of number exercising itself ... in all acts and the thoughts of men, in all handicrafts and music." "As soon as laws are necessary for men, they are no longer fit for freedom."

- 2450th anniversary of the birth of Socrates (470 BC – 399 BC, aged 71), great Greek philosopher.

Hiroshima: 17 April 2015, Bell of Peace (1964), The Greek inscription on the bell is Socrates' aphorism "Know yourself".

15 October - 2050th anniversary of the birth of Publius Vergilius Maro (15 Oct 70 BC – 21 Sep 19 BC, aged 50 years, 11 months and 6 days) in the farming village of Andes (now Virgilio), 6 km south of the city of Mantova (now Mantua, in Lombardia), 130 km southeast of Milano, in the Roman Republic province of Gallia Cisalpina, in northern Italy, to a wealthy equestrian farming family.

Vergilius was raised on his family's farm, and the Italian countryside, with its people, which influenced him early on, and was later echoed through his poetry. Vergilius died of fever at Brundisium harbor, Roman Empire (now Brindisi, Italia).

"Virgil's tomb" is found at the entrance of an ancient Roman tunnel ("grotta vecchia") in Piedigrotta, a district 3 km from the center of Napoli (Naples), near the Mergellina harbor, on the road heading north along the coast to Pozzuoli. It was a pilgrimage place for several centuries.

At Vergilius' death Horatius was 45 years, 9 months and 13 days.

Ovidius was 24 years, 6 months and 1 day, and published Heroides ("Epistulae Heroidum"), 14 poems about letters of mythological heroines to their absent lovers. Now Horatius became the most celebrated poet. Augustus, 44, who was a prolific letter-writer, offered him the job of his private secretary, but he declined the lucrative offer, being too busy with his poems. The Roman calendar was counted Ab urbe condita ("from the foundation of the city (Rome)", AUC)), in 753 BC; and it continued to be in use until the Anno Domini calendar was introduced in AD 525 = 1278 Ab urbe condita, therefore 19 BC = 734 Ab urbe condita (and 2018 = 2771 Ab urbe condita.

- 1900 years ago, in 80, in Rome the Amphitheatrum Flavium (recently incorrectly called Colosseum) was finished.

Rome: The south-west side of the Amphitheatrum Flavium (or Colosseum, 80 AD), with a flag throwing festival on December 8, 2011.

- 1650 years ago, in 330, Constantinople is officially named, and becomes the capital of the eastern Roman Empire. The Roman Emperor Constantin the Great founded 6 years earlier, in 324, this new capital in the east called New Rome, in 330 renamed Constantinople for about 1600 years, then, in the 1900s, to be changed to Istanbul.

Rome: The Amphitheatrum Flavium (Colosseum, 80 AD, left), the Arch of Constantine (315 AD, right), and a carabiniere wedding photo event.

- 1500th anniversary of the birth of Anicius Manlius Severinus Boëthius (circa 480 – 524, aged circa 44, Roman senator, consul, *magister officiorum*, and philosopher). In 524 he writes Consolation of Philosophy - one of the most popular and influential works of the Middle Ages.

1981 –

- 20 January - Ronald Wilson Reagan, 69.9, (6 Feb 1911 – 5 June 2004, aged 93.3) was inaugurated as the 40th President of the United States, for 8 years, from 20 Jan 1981 to 20 Jan 1989. Prior to the presidency, he was a Hollywood actor and trade union leader, before serving as the 33rd Governor of California from 1967 to 1975.

- 24 March - 300th anniversary of the birth of Georg Philipp Telemann (24 March 1681 – 25 June 1767, aged 86 years 3 months and 1 day, German composer and multi-instrumentalist).

- 12 August - the IBM Personal Computer is released.

- 450 years ago, in 1531, the Church of England breaks away from the Roman Catholic Church, and recognizes King Henry VIII as the head of the Church.

1982 –

- 22 February – 250th anniversary of the birth of George Washington (February 22, 1732 – December 14, 1799, aged 67.8), an American soldier, farmer, land investor, politician, and statesman who served from 1789 to 1797 as the first President of the United States, and became known as the "Father of the United States".

USA, Boston, 20 June 2015, Boston Public Garden (1837), statue of George Washington (1732-1799), by Thomas Ball in 1869.

31 March - 250th anniversary of the birth of Joseph Haydn (31 March 1732 – 31 May 1809, aged 77 years and 2 months, an Austrian composer of the Classical period. He was a friend and

mentor of Mozart (27 January 1756 – 5 December 1791, aged 35 years, 10 months and 8 days), a teacher of Beethoven (17 Dec 1770 – 26 March 1827, aged 56 years, 3 months and 9 days), and the older brother of composer Michael Haydn (14 Sep 1737 – 10 August 1806, aged 68.9). Joseph was born 5.5 years before Michael, and died 2.7 years after him; Michael Haydn also was a contemporaneous composer of Mozart (Michael was born 18.3 years before Mozart, and died 14.6 years after him).

- 500 years ago, in 1482, Campanus translated Euclid's The Elements from Arabic to Latin, and the first printed edition appeared in Venice in 1482.

- 4 October – 400 years ago, in 1582, Pope Gregory XIII, 80.7, (7 Jan 1502 – 10 April 1585, aged 83.2, Papacy 13 May1572 (at 70.3) – 10 April 1585 (for 12.9 years)) issues the Gregorian calendar (moved ahead 10 days, or shortened the year 1582 by 10 days). The last day of the Julian calendar was Thursday, 4 October 1582, and this was followed by the first day of the Gregorian calendar, Friday, 15 October 1582, which is in use today.

– 100 years ago, in 1882, Rodin, 42, designed a sculptural group depicting a couple entwined in each other's arms, their lips joined in a kiss, to be fitted onto the lower left door of The Gates of Hell (from Dante). Subsequently called The Kiss, the work would remain on The Gates 4 more years, until 1886.

The Kiss by Rodin, 42, 1882

– 50 years ago, in 1932 - BBC World Service starts broadcasting

Also, the positron (positive electron, the first known antiparticle of the electron) was discovered and photographed by the Nobel Laureate American Physicist Carl David Anderson, 27, (1905 – 1991, aged 86).

Chapter 5. 1983 - 1992

1983 –

- 3 September - 200 years ago, in 1783, the Treaty of Paris, where Great Britain recognized The U. S. A., formally ends the American Revolutionary War.

- November – The author, 40, and his younger son, 15.7, at Case Western Reserve University, in Cleveland.

Cleveland, Ohio, USA, in 1983 – M. Dediu (father, right, 40) and Horațiu Dediu (15.7, son, left, writing a mathematical proof), at Case Western Reserve University.

- 500th anniversary of the birth of Raphael (1483 – 1520, aged 37), great Italian painter and architect.

1984 –

- 700 years ago, in 1284, Peterhouse, the oldest college of the University of Cambridge, England, was founded by Hugo de Balsham, the Bishop of Ely.

- 700 years ago, in 1284, eyeglasses were invented in Venice.

- 300 years ago, in 1684, Calculus was independently developed by both Gottfried Wilhelm Leibniz, 38, and Sir Isaac Newton, 41, and used to formulate classical mechanics.

1985 –

- 1 January - the Internet's Domain Name System is created.

- 5 March - 300th anniversary of the birth of George Frideric Handel in Halle-upon-Saale (5 March 1685 – 14 April 1759, aged 74.1, burial place Westminster Abbey, London).

- 31 March - 300th anniversary of the birth of Johann Sebastian Bach (31 March 1685 – 28 July 1750, aged 65.3), German composer and musician. He is known for instrumental compositions such as the Brandenburg Concertos and the Goldberg Variations, as well as for vocal music such as the St. Matthew Passion. He is regarded as one of the greatest composers of all time.

Germany - 23 March 1978, Freibourg im Breisgau (1120 by Duke Berthold III of Zähringen (1085-1122), elevation 278 m, the south façade of Freiburger Münster (cathedral, 1200, 116 m, J. S. Bach (1685-1750) performed here).

26 October - 300th anniversary of the birth of Domenico Scarlatti in Napoli, (26 Oct 1685 – 23 July 1757, aged 71.7), son of Alessandro Scarlatti, 25.4, (2 May 1660 – 22 Oct 1725, aged 65.4). Handel, Bach and Domenico Scarlatti were contemporaneous: Handel was 26 days older than Bach, and Bach was 6 months and 1 day older than D. Scarlatti, but D. Scarlatti died 6 years, 11 months and 25 days after Bach, and Handel died 1 year, 8 months and 22 days after Domenico Scarlatti, therefore Handel was born first and died last at 74.1, Bach was born second but died first at 65.3, and Domenica Scarlatti was born the third, but died the second at 71.7.

- 30 November - 150th anniversary of the birth of Samuel Langhorne Clemens, pen name Mark Twain (30 Nov 1835 – 21 April 1910, aged 74.4), American writer, humorist, entrepreneur, publisher, and lecturer. He is considered the father of the American literature.

- 8 December - 2050th anniversary of the birth of Quintus Horatius Flaccus (8 Dec 65 BC – 27 Nov 8 BC, Rome, Roman Empire, aged 56 years 11 months and 19 days (11 days before 57), in Venusia (City of Venus, now Venosa, elevation 415 m, in the province of Potenza, 130 km east of Napoli, 300 km southeast of Rome, 620 km southeast of Andes (now Virgilio)), a small town between the border regions of Apulia and Lucania (Basilicata, the Vulture area), in the Samnite (south of Italy) in the Roman Republic. Images of his childhood setting, and references to it, are found throughout his poems.

At Horatius' birth, Vergilius was 5 years, 1 month and 23 days.

At Horatius' death Ovidius was 35 years, 8 months and 7 days.

- 1700 years ago, in 285, Diocletian (22 Dec 244 – 3 Dec 311, aged 66.9, Roman emperor for 21 years: 284 – 305) splits the Roman Empire into Eastern and Western Empires.

- 500th anniversary of the birth of Tiziano (Titian, 1485 – 1576, aged 91), famous Italian (Venetian) painter.

- Mikhail Sergeyevich Gorbachev, 54, becomes the eighth and last leader of the Soviet Union, as General Secretary of the governing Communist Party of the Soviet Union, for 6 years, from 1985 until 1991. He started and implemented radical good changes, eliminating Communism from the Soviet Union and Eastern Europe, and ending the Soviet Union.

Italy, Venezia: The central part of the east façade of Sansovino's Libreria (1537 – 1591) with Biblioteca Marciana (with Tiziano's and Tintoretto's paintings).

1986 –

- 25 January - 250th anniversary of the birth of Joseph-Louis Lagrange (born Giuseppe Lodovico Lagrangia or Giuseppe Ludovico De la Grange Tournier, in Torino, Italia, 25 January 1736 – Paris, 10 April 1813, Paris, aged 77.2) Italian mathematician and astronomer, who made significant contributions to the fields of analysis, number theory, and both classical and celestial mechanics. In 1766, on the recommendation of Euler, 59, and d'Alembert, 49, Lagrange, 30, succeeded Euler as the director of mathematics at the Prussian Academy of Sciences in Berlin, Prussia, where he stayed for over twenty years, producing volumes of work and winning several prizes of the French Academy of Sciences. In 1787, at age 51, he moved from Berlin to Paris, and became a member of the French Academy of Sciences. He remained in France until the end of his life.

- 24 May - 300th anniversary of the birth of Daniel Gabriel Fahrenheit (24 May 1686 – 16 September 1736, aged 50.3), Dutch-German-Polish physicist, inventor, and scientific instrument maker. He invented the mercury-in-glass thermometer (first practical, accurate thermometer), and Fahrenheit scale (first standardized temperature scale to be widely used).

- 19 September - 1900th anniversary of the birth of Antonius Pius (19 Sep 86 – 7 March 161, aged 74.5, Roman Emperor for 22.6 years: 11 July 138 – 7 March 161). From a senatorial family, Antoninus held various offices during the reign of emperor Hadrian, acquiring favor which saw him adopted as Hadrian's son and successor shortly before Hadrian's death. He acquired the name Pius after his accession to the throne, because he compelled the Senate to deify his adoptive father Hadrian, and because he had saved senators sentenced to death by Hadrian in his later years. His reign is notable for the peaceful state of the Empire, with no major revolts or military incursions during this time, and for his governing without ever leaving Italy. A successful military campaign in southern Scotland early in his reign resulted in the construction of the Antonine Wall. Antoninus was an effective administrator, leaving his successors a large surplus in the treasury, expanding free access to drinking water throughout the Empire, encouraging conformity with standards, and facilitating the enfranchisement of freed slaves. He died of illness in 161, and was succeeded by his adopted sons Marcus Aurelius and Lucius Verus as co-emperors. His rule of 22.6 years was the only one in which the Roman Empire did not fight in a war.

- 500 years ago, in 1486, Botticelli, 41, painted The Birth of Venus.

Botticelli, 41, 1486, The Birth of Venus

- 28 October – 100 years ago, in 1886, The Statue of Liberty (Liberty Enlightening the World; French: La Liberté éclairant le monde) was dedicated. It is a sculpture (46 m, from ground 93 m) on Liberty Island in New York Harbor in New York City, in the United States. The copper statue, a gift from the people of France to the people of the United States, was designed by French sculptor Frédéric Auguste Bartholdi and built by Gustave Eiffel.

- 18 November - 200th anniversary of the birth of Carl Maria von Weber (18 Nov 1786 – 5 June 1826, aged 39.5, German composer, conductor, pianist, guitarist and critic). He was a paternal half-cousin of Constanze Mozart.

- 13 December – 600th anniversary of Donatello's birth (1386 – 13 Dec 1466, aged 80, great Italian sculptor, teacher of Verrocchio).

- December – the author is in New York City.

USA, Dec 1986, New York City, 341 9th Ave (at W 30th St), the author (43.1) near the United States Post Office, "Neither snow, nor rain, nor heat, nor gloom of night, stays these couriers from the swift completion of their appointed rounds".

- 350 years ago, in 1636, Harvard University was founded in Cambridge, Massachusetts, north of Boston.

USA, Cambridge, 23 September 2009, on the campus of Harvard University (1636) in Cambridge, The Harry Elkins Widener (1885-1912 (died on Titanic)) Memorial Library (1915, Beaux-Arts architecture, 3.5 M of books).

- 100 years ago, in 1886, Karl Benz sells the first commercial automobile.

1987 –

- 5 July - 300 years ago, in 1687, Isaac Newton, 44.5, published Philosophiae Naturalis Principia Mathematica.

- 23 September - 2050th anniversary of the birth of Gaius Octavius, later Augustus (23 Sep 63 BC – 19 Aug 14, aged 75 years 10 month and 27 days (just 35 days before 76), being the first Roman emperor for 40 years and 7 months. Burial place: Mausoleum of Augustus in Rome.

- 500 years ago, in 1487, Leonardo da Vinci, 35, drew L'Uomo Vitruviano (the Vitruvian Man, now at Accademia in Venice), which is regarded as a cultural icon, being reproduced on the euro coin, textbooks, etc. Vitruvius was an ancient Roman architect, interested in the proportions of the human body.

- 350 years ago, in 1637, Pierre de Fermat, 30, (November 1607 – 12 Jan 1665, aged 57.2, French mathematician) formulated his Last Theorem in number theory, unsolved for 358 years, until 1995.

1988 –

- 900 years ago, in 1088, University of Bologna, Italy, was founded. It is the oldest university in continuous operation.

- 100 years ago, in 1888, The American Mathematical Society was founded.

- 50 years ago, in 1938, instant coffee was invented in the U.S.

Italy, 12 May 1978, Bologna (1000 BC, 140 km², elevation 54 m, metro population 1 M, the capital and largest city of the Emilia-Romagna region in Northern Italy, with the oldest university in the world, University of Bologna, founded in 1088), west of Piazza di Porta San Donato, from Via Zamboni looking east to the north façade of the Università degli Studi di Bologna, Dipartimento di Matematica, Istituto di Matematica.

1989 –

- 7 January - the 124th Emperor of Japan, Hirohito, died (29 April 1901 – 7 Jan 1989, aged 87.6, reigning for 62 years, from 25 December 1926 (age 25.6), until his death on 7 January 1989. He was succeeded by his eldest son, Akihito, 55, (born 23 Dec 1933).).

- 20 January - George Herbert Walker Bush, 64.4, (12 June 1924 – 30 Nov 2018, aged 94.4) was inaugurated as the 41st President of the United States, for 4 years, from 20 Jan 1989 to 20 Jan 1993. Prior to assuming the presidency, he served as the 43rd Vice President of the United States, with President Ronald Reagan, from 1981 to 1989.

16 March - 200th anniversary of the birth of Georg Simon Ohm (16 March 1789 – 6 July 1854, aged 65.3), German physicist and mathematician, who did his research with the new electrochemical cell, invented by Italian scientist Alessandro Volta. Using equipment of his own creation, Ohm found that there is a direct proportionality between the potential difference (voltage) applied across a conductor, and the resultant electric current. This relationship is known as Ohm's law.

21 August – 200th anniversary of the birth of Augustin-Louis Cauchy (21 August 1789 – 23 May 1857, aged 67.7), French mathematician, engineer and physicist, who made pioneering contributions to several branches of mathematics, including: mathematical analysis and continuum mechanics. He founded complex analysis, and the study of permutation groups in abstract algebra.

- 22 December - after a week of bloody demonstrations, Ion Iliescu (born 1930) takes over as president of Romania, ending the communist dictatorship, after 45.3 years.

- 1000 years ago, in 989, Pax Dei et Treuga Dei (Peace and Truce of God) was formed - the first movement of the Roman Catholic Church (which now has 1.3 B members), using spiritual means, to limit private wars, and the first movement in medieval Europe to control society through non-violent means.

- 500 years ago, in 1489 - 1490, Leonardo da Vinci, 37, painted Lady with an Ermine, the lady being Cecilia Gallerani.

- 200 years ago, in 1789, George Washington was elected the first President of the United States; he served 2 terms until 1797.

- 200 years ago, in 1789, Antoine Lavoisier discovered the law of conservation of mass, the basis for chemistry, and modern chemistry begins.

- 100 years ago, in 1889, Eiffel Tower (324 m) was inaugurated in Paris. Also, aspirin was patented.

Paris: The south-west façade of Palais de Chaillot (1937, left) and the north-west side of Tour Eiffel (1889, 324 m), from Place du Trocadéro et du 11 Novembre.

- 50 years ago, in 1939, the uranium atom first split takes place at Columbia University, U.S.A.

Leonardo da Vinci, 38, 1490, Lady with an Ermine (the lady being Cecilia Gallerani)

1990 –

- 4550 years ago, in 2560 BC, King Khufu of Egypt completed the Great Pyramid of Giza, 146.5 m.

Egypt, the upper part of the Great Pyramid of Giza, 2560 BC, 146.5 m.

- 2450th anniversary of the birth of Democritus (c. 460 BC – c. 370 BC, aged c. 90, influential pre-Socratic philosopher, mathematician and astronomer, who formulated an atomic theory of the universe, father of modern science) announces, when he was 75, in 385 BC (when Plato was 43), that the Milky Way (Via Lactea, which includes the Solar System, which is about 27,000 light-years from the Galactic Center) is a concentration of many distant stars (200 - 400 billions).

- 2300th anniversary of the birth of Aristarchus of Samos, (c. 310 BC — c. 230 BC, aged c. 80), Greek mathematician and astronomer, who sustained that Earth rotates on its axis, and revolves around the Sun (Heliocentrism).

Japan, 19 Nov 2008, looking south to a blooming tree (left) after the mid of November and the author (65, invited at TDU), near an artesian fountain in the central park from the Inzai (Chiba) campus of Tokyo Denki University (TDU), at sunset; the building to the right is the Library.

- 750th anniversary of the birth of Cimabue (1240 – 1302, aged 62, Italian painter and designer of mosaics from Florence).

- 500 years ago, in 1490, Leonardo da Vinci, 38, painted La belle ferronnière.

La belle ferronnière, 1490, by Leonardo da Vinci, 38.

– 12 November – 150th anniversary of the birth, in 1840, of François Auguste René Rodin, known as Auguste Rodin (12 Nov 1840 - 17 November 1917, aged 77 years and 5 days) in the Rue de l'Arbalète, in the 12th arrondissement (present 5th arrondissement), a working-class area of Paris. His father was Jean-Baptiste Rodin, 37, (1803 – 1883, aged 80, clerk in a police station, and then police inspector), and his mother Marie Rodin (circa 1806 – 1871, aged circa 65) August was the second child, after his sister Maria (1838 – 1862, aged 24).

- 14 November – 150th anniversary of the birth, in 1840, two days after August Rodin, of Claude Monet (14 Nov 1840 – 5 Dec 1926, aged 86 years and 3 weeks, French painter).

The Panthéon (1758 - 1790, 83 m height, mausoleum in the Latin Quarter in Paris, modeled on the Pantheon (25 BC, 126 AD) in Rome), seen from Rue Soufflot.

- 50 years ago, in 1940, Neptunium is synthesized.
Also, the 40-hour work week goes into effect in the U.S.A.

1991 –

- 2500 years ago, in 509 BC, the expulsion of the last King of Rome, and the founding of the Roman Republic (traditional date) took place.

- 1 August - 700 years ago, in 1291, Confederatio Helvetica (Switzerland) was founded on the unity of the communes of Uri, Schwyz, and Unterwalden.

Geneva, on Pont du Mont Blanc (1862, 1965, 252 m X 26.8 m, over Rhône river), going northwest, Les Bergues Hotel (1834) (center).

- 450th anniversary of the birth of El Greco (Domenikos Theotokopoulos) (1541 – 1614, aged 73), Greek-Spanish painter, sculptor and architect.

- 400 years ago, in 1591, the first flush toilet was introduced by Sir John Harrington of England, the design published under the title 'The Metamorphosis of Ajax'.

1992 –

29 February – 200th anniversary of the birth of Gioachino Rossini (29 February 1792 – 13 November 1868, aged 76.7, Italian composer who wrote 39 operas, as well as some sacred music, songs, chamber music, and piano pieces; he was a precocious composer of operas, and he made his debut at age 18).

- 2500 years ago, in 508 BC, the democracy was instituted in Athens, Greece.

- 800 years ago, in 1192, in Japan: Minamoto no Yoritomo is appointed Sei-i Taishōgun, or shōgun for short. He is the first of a long line of military dictators to bear this title. The institution would last for 721 years, until 1913.

Japan: the author in a delightful classical Japanese restaurant, with exquisite Japanese food and service, in Tsukuba Science City (founded in 1962), in Ibaraki Prefecture, 60 km north-east of Tokyo.

- 12 October – 500 years ago, in 1492, Christopher Columbus, 41.9, (31 Oct 1451, Republic of Genoa – 20 May 1506, Spain, aged 54.6, Italian explorer and navigator) landed in the Americas from Spain.

– 500 years ago, in 1492, Muhammad XII or Boabdil's (the 22nd and last ruler of the Emirate of Granada in Iberia) surrender of Granada marked the end of the Spanish Reconquista (after 781 years (711 – 1492) of Arab occupation, called Al-Andalus or Muslim Spain).

200 years ago, in 1792, The New York Stock & Exchange Board was founded – now, after 226 years, it is the world's largest stock exchange, with a market capitalization of its listed companies of over $21 T.

USA, New York: On W 32nd St, looking east, before Ave of the Americas and Broadway: Empire State Building (center back) Manhattan Mall (left), Radisson Martinique on Broadway Hotel (center down).

Chapter 6. 1993 - 2002

1993 –

28 March – 1800 years ago, in 193, the 64 days rule of Emperor Didius Julianus (2 Feb 137 – 1 June 193, aged 56.3, reign 28 March 193 – 1 June 193) of the Roman Empire began.

- 500th anniversary of the birth of Paracelsus (11 November or 17 December 1493 in Einsiedeln, Switzerland – 24 September 1541 in Salzburg, Austria, aged 47.7), Swiss physician and botanist.

- 500th anniversary of the birth of François Rabelais (1493 – 1553, aged 60), French writer, physician, humanist, and Greek scholar.

- 400 years ago, in 1593, Galileo Galilei invented the thermometer.

1994 –

- 2200 years ago, in 206 BC, Han Dynasty was established in China, after the death of Qin Shi Huang; China in this period officially becomes a Confucian state, and opens trading connections with the West, i.e. the Silk Road.

- 3 January - 2100th anniversary of the birth of Marcus Tullius Cicero (3 Jan 106 BC – 7 Dec 43 BC, aged 63.9, Roman statesman, orator and philosopher, who served as consul in the year 63 BC). Cicero's quote: Gratitude is not only the greatest of virtues, but the parent of all the others.

- 5 July – Jeff Bezos (30.5) founded the company Amazon.

- 21 November - 300th anniversary of the birth of François-Marie Arouet (21 November 1694 – 30 May 1778, aged 83.5), known by his nom de plume Voltaire, a French writer, historian and philosopher famous for his wit, and his advocacy of freedom of religion, freedom of speech, and separation of church and state. Voltaire was a versatile and prolific writer, producing works in almost every literary form, including plays, poems, novels, essays, and historical and scientific works. He wrote more than 20,000 letters, and more than 2,000 books and pamphlets.

Solzhenitsyn, 76, following the reinstatement of his citizenship in 1990, after the collapse of the U.S.S.R., returns home, settles near Moscow, where he would live the rest of his life.

1995 –

– 600th anniversary of the birth of Beato Angelico (Fra Angelico, born Guido di Pietro; c. 1395 – February 18, 1455, aged c. 59.5), Italian painter, with his famous painting "Annunciation" (c. 1430, when he was 35) in Diocesan Museum in Cortona.

- 100 years ago, in 1895, Wilhelm Röntgen identifies x-rays.

1996 –

- 2000th anniversary of the birth of Lucius Annaeus Seneca (4 BC - 65 AD, aged 68), Roman Stoic philosopher, statesman and dramatist.

- 31 March – 400th anniversary of the birth of Birth of René Descartes (Renatus Cartesius; adjectival form: "Cartesian"; 31 March 1596 – 11 February 1650, aged 53.9), French mathematician, philosopher, and scientist. He is the father of analytical geometry and of modern Western philosophy.

14 May – 200 years ago, in 1796, Edward Jenner, 46.99, (17 May 1749 – 26 Jan 1823, aged 73.6, English physician and scientist) administers the first smallpox vaccination; smallpox killed an estimated 400,000 Europeans each year during the 18th century, including five reigning monarchs.

- 100 years ago, in 1896, The Olympic Games were revived in Athens.

1997 –

- 3300th anniversary of the birth of Rameses II (1303 – 1213, aged 90), Pharaoh of Egypt for 66 years: 1279 (age 24) – 1213 BC (age 90)).

- 1300 years ago, in 697 - founding of the Republic of Venice (Serenissima Reppublica di Venezia, 697 – 1797, for 1,100 years powerful maritime republic centered in Venezia).

Venezia: Libreria (left), San Theodore Column, Palazzo Ducale, Lion of Venice Column (center) on Riva degli Schiavoni street.

– 600th anniversary of the birth of Paolo Uccello (1397 – 10 December 1475, aged 78), born Paolo di Dono, Italian painter and mathematician, who is remembered for his pioneering work on visual perspective in art.

1998 –

- 600th anniversary of the birth of Johannes Gensfleisch zur Laden zum Gutenberg (1398 – 3 February 1468, aged 69), known as Gutenberg, German blacksmith, goldsmith, printer, and publisher, who introduced printing to Europe with the printing press.

- 500 years ago, in 1498, Leonardo da Vinci, 46, who was commissioned in 1495, to paint the mural Il Cenacolo or L'Ultima Cena (The Last Supper) in Milano, for the refectory of the Convent of Santa Maria delle Grazie – finished it after 3 years. It is the most reproduced religious painting of all time.

1999 –

- 1 January - the euro is established and becomes the official currency of the Eurozone, which consists of 19 of the 28-member states of the European Union.

- 500 years ago, in 1499, Michelangelo, 24, completed Pietà, one of the world's great masterpieces of sculpture, which is now located in St. Peter's Basilica in Vatican. In November 1497, when Michelangelo was 22.6, the French ambassador to the Holy See, Cardinal Jean de Bilhères-Lagraulas, 62, (1435 – 6 August 1499, Rome, aged 64, buried in the Chapel of St. Petronilla in St. Peter's Basilica), commissioned him to carve a Pietà, a sculpture showing the Virgin Mary grieving over the body of Jesus, for the Chapel of St. Petronilla, the chapel of the King of France in St. Peter's Basilica in Vatican. In August 1498, when Michelangelo was 23.4, the contract for Pietà was agreed upon, and he began to carve the Rome Pietà, for about one year.

- 20 May - 200th anniversary of the birth of Honoré de Balzac (20 May 1799 – 18 August 1850, aged 51.2, French novelist and playwright).

- 6 June – 200th anniversary of the birth of Alexander Pushkin (6 June 1799, Boldino, Russia – 1837, aged 38), great Russian poet, the founder of modern Russian literary language.

30 November - Professor Germán Arciniegas passed away of pneumonia, in Bogotá, Colombia, (6 Dec 1900 – 30 Nov 1999, aged 98 years 11 months and 24 days (just 6 days before his 99th birthday). For some time before passing, he was blind and deaf, but he was still dictating his twice-monthly column. Professor Arciniegas left a monumental work as a historian, author (over 70 books), essayist (over 15,000 essays and articles), diplomat, professor, statesman, and journalist. Colombian President Andres Pastrana decreed three days of national mourning for Professor Arciniegas.

- 200 years ago, in 1799, Rosetta Stone was discovered by Napoleon's troops.

- 100 years ago, in 1899, the German mathematician David Hilbert, 37, presented Foundations of Geometry, the first complete set of geometry axioms since Euclid, over 2150 years ago.

Rome, Vatican, Basilica di San Pietro (1506): the sculpture in Carrara marble Pietà (1498–1499, moved to the first chapel, on the right, around 1750) by Michelangelo Buonarroti (1475 – 1564). It is the only piece Michelangelo ever signed.

2000 –

- 2000, which is the last year of the 2nd millennium, and the 100th and last year of the 20th century, was designated as the World Mathematical Year.

- 17 January - 400th anniversary of the birth of Pedro Calderón de la Barca (17 Jan 1600 – 25 May 1681, aged 81.3, Spanish dramatist, poet and writer).

- 8 February - 300th anniversary of the birth of Daniel Bernoulli (8 February1700 – 17 March 1782, aged 82.1), Swiss mathematician and physicist, one of the many prominent mathematicians in the Bernoulli family. He is remembered for his applications of mathematics to mechanics, especially fluid mechanics, and for his work in probability and statistics. His name is commemorated in the Bernoulli's principle, an example of the conservation of energy, which describes the mathematics of the mechanism underlying the operation of two important technologies of the 20th century: the carburetor and the airplane wing.

-13 July - 2100th anniversary of the birth of Gaius Julius Caesar (13 July 100 BC – 15 March 44 BC, aged 55.6), usually called Julius Caesar, a Roman politician and general who played a critical role in the events that led to the transformation of the Roman Republic into the Roman Empire).

- 25 December – 1200 years ago, in 800, Charlemagne, 58.7, was crowned Holy Roman Emperor. With his crowning, Charlemagne's kingdom is officially recognized by the Papacy as the largest in Europe since the fall of the Western Roman Empire, more than 300 years ago. Also, gunpowder was invented around 800.

The marble statue of the French king Charlemagne (742-814), by Charles Antoine Coysevox (1640-1720) on the right side of the entrance of L'Église du Dôme (1708, 107 m, inspired by St. Peter's Basilica in Rome,1626) in the center of L'Hôtel National des Invalides (1678, founded by Louis XIV (1638–1715), in the 7th arrondissement, with military museums and monuments, and the burial site for Napoleon Bonaparte (1769-1821)). Napoleon was entombed under the Dôme of the Invalides, in a tomb made of red quartzite and resting on a green granite base, finished in 1861.

- 300 years ago, in 1700, the piano was invented.

2001 –

- 2001 is the 1st year of the 3rd millennium, and the 1st year of the 21st century.

- 20 January - George Walker Bush, 54.5, (born 6 July 1946, at the end of 2018 he was 72.5) was inaugurated as the 43rd President of the United States, for 8 years, from 20 Jan 2001 to 20 Jan 2009. He had previously served as the 46th Governor of Texas from 1995 to 2000. Bush was born in New Haven, Connecticut, and grew up in Texas.

- 27 November – 300th anniversary of the birth of Anders Celsius (27 November 1701 – 25 April 1744, aged 42.4), Swedish mathematician, astronomer, and physicist. He founded the Uppsala Astronomical Observatory in 1741, and in 1742 proposed the Celsius temperature scale, which bears his name.

- A smaller bridge based on Leonardo's 499 years old design, from 1502, was constructed in Norway. In 1502, Leonardo, 50, sketched the design for the Golden Horn Bridge – a single span 240 m bridge over the Horn (a prominent body of water, horn-shaped estuary, that joins Bosphorus Strait at the immediate point where the strait meets the Sea of Marmara, thus forming to the south a narrow, isolated peninsula, the tip of which is Old ancient Byzantium and Constantinople, now Istanbul. Leonardo produced this drawing of a single span bridge as part of a civil engineering project for Ottoman Sultan Bayezid II of Constantinople. The bridge was intended to span an inlet at the mouth of the Bosporus known as the Golden Horn. Bayezid did not pursue the project, because he believed that such a construction was impossible. Leonardo's vision was resurrected in 2001, when a smaller bridge based on his design was constructed in Norway.

2002 –

- 26 February - 200th anniversary of the birth of Victor Hugo (26 Feb 1802 – 22 May 1885, aged 83.2, French poet, novelist, and dramatist). There is a statue of Victor Hugo in Rome, Italy. It is across from the Museo Carlo Bilotti on Viale Fiorello La Guardia.

- 100 years ago, in 1902, Willis Carrier, 26, invents the first modern electrical air conditioning unit.

The upper part of the western façade of Cathédrale Notre Dame de Paris (1163 – 1345, 90 m), on the south-eastern part of the Île de la Cité, which is considered the center of Paris, in the fourth arrondissement. The organ has 7,374 pipes, with about 900 classified as historical. It has 110 real stops, five 56-key manuals and a 32-key pedalboard; it is now fully computerized. The Towers at Notre-Dame contain five church bells. The great bourdon bell, Emmanuel, from 1681, 13 t, is located in the South Tower (right).

Chapter 7. 2003 - 2012

2003 –

- 600 years ago, in 1403, the Yongle Emperor (the third emperor of the Ming dynasty, for 22 years, 1402-1424) moved the capital of China from Nanjing to Beijing.

- 600 years ago, in 1403, the settlement of the Canary Islands (in the Atlantic Ocean, 100 km west of Morocco) signals the beginning of the Spanish Empire, which will exist for more than 500 years.

- 400 years ago, in 1603, Accademia Nazionale dei Lincei was founded in Rome.

Rome: Accademia Nazionale dei Lincei (1603) in Villa Farnesina (1510). The author was invited to give a lecture here in 1978.

- 100 years ago, in 1903 – the first controlled heavier-than-air flight of the Wright Brothers.

1 Dec 2007, Washington, D.C. (1790): the 1903 Wright Flyer airplane and the author (64), at The National Air and Space Museum (1976) of the Smithsonian Institution, between Jefferson Dr SW and Independence Ave SW.

2004 –

- 20 July – 700th anniversary of the birth of Francesco Petrarca (20 July 1304, Arezzo, Italy – 19 July 1374, Arquà, Italy aged 69.99 (just one day before 70), scholar and poet of Renaissance Italy, influenced by Horatius' poetry, who was the founder of Humanism. His rediscovery of Cicero's letters is considered the beginning of the 14th-century Renaissance.

Italy, 8 Sep 1977, Sophia Dediu (34) at Cortona (20 km southeast of Arezzo (circa 1500 BC, 343 km², elevation 494 m, population 23,000)), the southwest façade and entrance of Il Palazzone di Cortona (1521-1527, 2 km southeast of Cortona).

    - 500 years ago, in 1504, Michelangelo, 29, completed, after 3 years of work, his most famous work, the statue of David. In 1501 he received a commission, from the consuls of the Guild of Wool, to complete an unfinished project begun 41 years earlier, in 1460, by Agostino di Duccio (1418 – 1481, aged 63, Italian sculptor): a colossal statue of Carrara marble portraying David, as a symbol of Florentine freedom, to be placed on the gable of Florence Cathedral. However, Leonardo da Vinci, 52, and Botticelli, 59, were invited to be in a committee formed to relocate, against Michelangelo's will, his statue of David, from the gable of Florence Cathedral to, ultimately, the Piazza della Signoria, in front of the Palazzo Vecchio. Now it stands in the Galleria dell'Accademia di Firenze (1784, 1 km north of Palazzo Vecchio), while a replica occupies its place in the Piazza della Signoria.

- 200 years ago, in 1804, the world population reached 1 billion, and the first steam locomotive begins operation.

2005 –

- 27 September – The author with his wife are in Helsinki.

Finland in 2005: the author and his wife (both 62) in a suburb of Helsinki, 10 km north-east from the center; on a large balcony of an apartment, with a nice view of a small island in the Baltic Sea.

500 years ago, in 1505, Raphael, 22, painted The Small Cowper Madonna.

The Small Cowper Madonna by Raphael, 22, in 1505, now at the National Gallery of Art in Washington, D.C.

2006 –

- 2500 years ago, in 494 BC, Pericles was born (494 BC – 429 BC, aged 65, a prominent and influential Greek statesman, orator, general and patron of the arts of Athens during the Golden Age — specifically 31 years (460 BC (age 34) – 429 BC (age 65)), the time between the Persian war (499 BC – 449 BC, 50 years, the last 11 years under Pericles), and the Peloponnesian war (431 BC – 404 BC, 27 years, the first 2 years under Pericles). Quotes: "What you leave behind is not what is engraved in stone monuments, but what is woven into the lives of others." "Just because you do not take an interest in politics doesn't mean politics won't take an interest in you." "Freedom is the sure possession of those alone who have the courage to defend it.").

- 17 January - 300th anniversary of the birth of Benjamin Franklin (January 17, 1706, on Milk Street in Boston, Massachusetts Bay, English America – April 17, 1790, aged 84 years and 3 months), an American polymath and one of the Founding Fathers of the United States. Franklin was a leading author, printer, political theorist, politician, freemason, postmaster, scientist, inventor, humorist, civic activist, statesman, and diplomat. As a scientist he is known for his discoveries and theories regarding electricity. As an inventor, he is known for the lightning rod, bifocals, and the Franklin stove, among other inventions. He founded many civic organizations, including Philadelphia's fire department and the University of Pennsylvania. Benjamin Franklin quote: "An investment in knowledge pays the best interest". "Remember not only to say the right thing in the right place, but, far more difficult still, to leave unsaid the wrong thing at the tempting moment.'

Benjamin's father Josiah had in total 17 children, with two wives.

USA, Boston: a view of the north-east part of Boston, from Cambridge, over Charles River Basin. Federal Reserve Bank Building (187 m, left), and other tall buildings in the financial district.

- 500 years ago, in 1506, Leonardo da Vinci, 54, finished, after 3 years of work, in Florence, the painting in oil, on a poplar panel, Mona Lisa (or La Gioconda). It is the most famous portrait, now at Louvre Museum, Paris, France.

- 6 June - 400th anniversary of the birth of Pierre Corneille (6 June 1606 – 1 October 1684, aged 78.3), French tragedian, one of the three great seventeenth-century French dramatists, along with Molière and Racine.

- 3 November – with the occasion of the 200th anniversary of the birth of John Stuart Mill (20 May 1806 – 8 May 1873, aged 66.9 (12 days before 67), British philosopher, political economist, and civil servant), the International Philosophical Conference "John Stuart Mill, 1806 – 2006" took place.

Oxford Philosopher J. R. Lucas (right, born 18 June 1932, age 74.5), and M. Dediu (3 days before 63), on November 3, 2006, at the International Philosophical Conference "John Stuart Mill, 1806 – 2006".

Oxford Philosopher J. R. Lucas (right, born 18 June 1932, age 74.5), and M. Dediu (3 days before 63), on November 3, 2006, at the International Philosophical Conference "John Stuart Mill, 1806 – 2006".

Paris in 2013: the author (70) near the statue of Pierre Corneille (1606 – 1684, aged 78.3, poet and dramatist, the creator of French classical tragedy (Le Cid, Horace, Cinna, La Place royale), one of the three great 17th century French dramatists, with Molière (1622 – 1673, aged 51) and Racine (1639 – 1699, aged 60)) and Paroisse Saint-Étienne-du-Mont (center, 510, 1222, 1328, 1492-1626) – Catholic church, northeast of the Panthéon (right) with the tombs of Blaise Pascal (1623 – 1662, aged 39, mathematician, physicist, philosopher, inventor and writer) and Jean-Baptiste Racine.

– 15 July – 400th anniversary of the birth of Rembrandt Harmenszoon van Rijn (15 July 1606 – 4 October 1669, aged 63 years 2 months and 20 days), in Leiden (elevation 0 m, 35 km southwest of Amsterdam, and 15 km northeast of The Hague), Dutch Republic (now the Netherlands) – both parents were 38 years old. Rembrandt produced a total of 772 paintings, drawings and prints (the number of paintings is 324).

Rubens was 29 years and 17 days.

- 100 years ago, in 1906, Brazilian inventor Alberto Santos-Dumont takes off and flies his biplane 14-bis to a crowd in Paris, being the first manned powered flight to be publicly witnessed.

Copy of Mona Lisa (or La Gioconda, detail), 1506, by Leonardo da Vinci, 54.

2007 –

- 25 February - 300th anniversary of the birth of Carlo Goldoni in Venezia (25 Feb 1707 - 6 Feb 1793, Paris, aged 85.9, 19 days before 86, a famous playwright).

- 15 April – 300th anniversary of the birth of Leonhard Euler (15 April 1707, Basel, Switzerland – 18 September 1783, Saint Petersburg, Russia, aged 76.4), Swiss mathematician, physicist, astronomer, logician and engineer, who made important discoveries in infinitesimal calculus and graph theory, topology and analytic number theory. He also introduced much of the modern mathematical terminology and notation, particularly for mathematical analysis, such as the notion of a mathematical function. He is also known for his work in mechanics, fluid dynamics, optics, astronomy, and music theory.

– 7 December - a red chalk sketch, about 450 years old, for the dome of St Peter's Basilica, possibly the last made by Michelangelo before his death, in 1564, was discovered in the Vatican archives. It is extremely rare, since he destroyed his designs later in life. The sketch is a partial plan for one of the radial columns of the cupola drum of Saint Peter's.

2008 –

- 706 years ago, in 1302, Dante Alighieri, 37, (30 May 1265, Firenze, Italy – 14 Sep 1321, Ravenna, Italy, aged 56.3), the great Renaissance poet, was exiled from Firenze. He was pardoned now, in 2008, by Firenze (Florence) – from where he was exiled on pain of death in 1302 (when he was 37), 706 years ago.

– 500th anniversary of the birth of Andrea Palladio (1508-1580, aged 72), important Italian architect.

- 500 years ago, in 1508, Leonardo da Vinci, 56, painted The Virgin and Child with St. Anne.

The Virgin and Child with St. Anne, by Leonardo da Vinci, 56, in 1508.

3 August - Aleksandr Solzhenitsyn passed away (11 Dec 1918 – 3 Aug 2008, aged 89.6). He was a great Russian writer, historian and mathematician, who significantly contributed to the collapse of the totalitarianism in the USSR and Eastern Europe.

- 26 November – The author (65) is at Tokyo Denki University.

The entrance to the Tokyo (in 2008) campus of Tokyo Denki University (TDU, private university founded 1907, chartered 1949)

__2009__ –

- 12 February - 200th anniversary of the birth of Charles Robert Darwin, (12 February 1809 – 19 April 1882, aged 73.2), English naturalist, geologist and biologist, best known for his contributions to the evolution theory. He had 10 children.

- 500 years ago, in 1509, Leonardo da Vinci, 57, prepared a series of drawings of regular solids in a skeletal form, to be engraved as plates for Pacioli's (62) book "De divina proportione", published in this year.

Also, in 1509, Michelangelo, 34, completed Ignudo fresco on the Sistine Chapel ceiling.

- 300 years ago, in 1709, The first piano was built by Bartolomeo Cristofori.

2010 –

- 3300 years ago, in 1290 BC, Sety I became the Pharaoh of Egypt (1290 BC – 1279 BC, 11 years).

4 January - 300th anniversary of the birth of Giovanni Battista Pergolesi (4 Jan 1710 – 16 March 1736, aged 26.2, Italian composer, violinist and organist; his best-known works include his Stabat Mater and the opera *La serva padrona* (*The Maid Turned Mistress*)).

23 January – the author (66.2) visits the Worcester Polytechnic Institute (WPI, 1865, private research university in Worcester, MA, USA, 6,000 students).

USA, Massachusetts, Worcester, 23 Jan 2010, the author (67.1) is at Stoddard Laboratories (left), Salisbury Laboratories (center) and Fuller Laboratories (right) at the Worcester Polytechnic Institute (WPI, 1865, private research university in Worcester, 6,000 students).

- 2900 years ago, in 890 BC, is the approximate date for the composition of the Iliad and the Odyssey by Homer.

- 2 September – 2500 years ago, in 490 BC, Phidippides runs the first marathon, seeking aid from Sparta for Athens, against Persia.

- 200 years ago, in 1810, Antonio Canova (1757 – 1822, aged 65, sculptor from Venezia) finished Venere (Venus) Italica, a carved Carrara marble sculpture, 1.75 m, commissioned by Napoleon Bonaparte (1769 – 1821, aged 52).

- 200th anniversary of the birth of Frédéric Chopin (1810-1849, aged 39).

Venere (Venus) Italica, 1810, by Antonio Canova (1757 – 1822, aged 65, sculptor from Venezia), a carved Carrara marble sculpture, 1.75 m, commissioned by Napoleon Bonaparte (1769 – 1821, aged 52).

2011

— 1800th anniversary of the birth of Diophantus of Alexandria (211 – 295, aged 84), mathematician, who was the author of a series of books called Arithmetica, many of which are now lost. He is called "the father of algebra".

30 July - 500th anniversary of the birth of Giorgio Vasari (30 July 1511 – 27 June 1574, aged 62.9), Italian painter, architect, writer, and historian, most famous today for his "Lives of the Most Excellent Painters, Sculptors, and Architects", considered the foundation of art-historical writing.
Also, in 1511, Michelangelo, 36, completed The Creation of Man (1510-1511), a fresco on the vault of the Sistine Chapel.

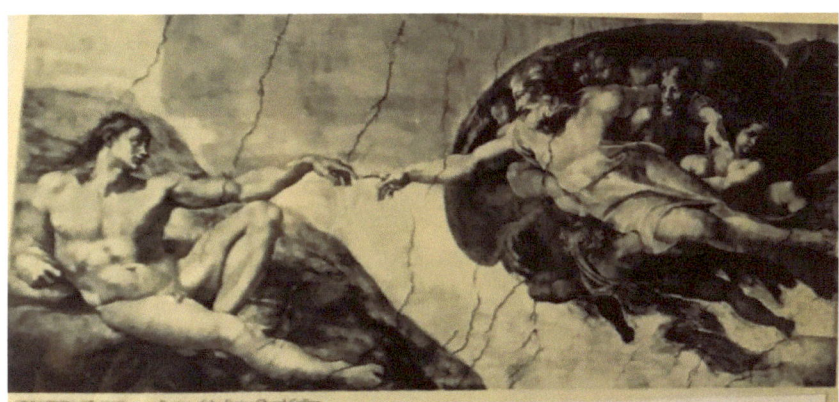

Michelangelo, 36, completed The Creation of Man (1510-1511), a fresco on the vault of the Sistine Chapel. The Lord's gesture is superb, as His mighty arm becomes the channel for the life force. Adam's arm resting passively on his knee. These two figures are the best known of all Sistine paintings.

25 October – 200th anniversary of the birth of Évariste Galois (25 October 1811 – 31 May 1832, aged 20.6), great French mathematician. While still in his teens, he was able to determine a necessary and sufficient condition for a polynomial to be solvable by radicals, thereby solving a problem standing for 350 years. His work laid the foundations for Galois theory and group theory, two

major branches of abstract algebra, and the subfield of Galois connections.

- November – The author is in Rome.

Roma in 2011: the author (68) is at Pantheon (126 AD) and the Fontana del Pantheon in Piazza della Rotonda. Commissioned in 27 BC by Marcus Agrippa (63 BC -12 BC), and rebuilt by Emperor Hadrian (76–138, Emperor 117-138), in about 126.

– Davinciite, a recently described mineral recognized in 2011 by the International Mineralogical Association, is named in honor of Leonardo.

2012 –

- 28 May – 200 years ago, in 1812, the Treaty of Bucharest between the Ottoman Empire and the Russian Empire, was signed, in Hanul lui Manuc (Manuc's Inn) in Bucharest, and ratified on 5 July 1812, at the end of the Russo-Turkish War. Under its terms, the eastern half of the Principality of Moldavia, between Prut and Dniester Rivers, with an area of 45,630 km^2 (Bessarabia), was ceded by the Ottoman Empire (to which Moldavia was a vassal) to Russia.

Also, Russia obtained trading rights on the Danube. A truce was signed (Article 8 of the Treaty) with the rebelling Serbs, and autonomy given to Serbia. The treaty, signed by the Russian commander Mikhail Kutuzov, was ratified by Alexander I of Russia 13 days before Napoleon's invasion of Russia.

- 28 June - 300th anniversary of the birth of Jean-Jacques Rousseau (28 June 1712 – 2 July 1778, aged 66 years and 4 days, Genevan philosopher, writer and composer).

- 30 August - launch from Cape Canaveral of the racket Atlas V, with the twin Radiation Belt Storm Probes (RBSP). There are five instruments aboard the RBSP. One of them is the space weather instrument RBSP Ion Composition Experiment known as RBSPICE. Each RBSP spacecraft weighs about 660 kilograms and carries an identical set of five instrument suites that will examine the radiation belts surrounding Earth.

- October – 500 years ago, in 1512, Michelangelo, 37.6, finished the painting of the Sistine Chapel. In February 1508 he was summoned to Rome by Pope Julius II, 64.2, who asked him to paint the ceiling of the Sistine Chapel, which he finished after 4.6 years, in October 1512. Michelangelo was originally commissioned to paint the Twelve Apostles on the triangular pendentives that supported the ceiling, and to cover the central part of the ceiling with ornament. Michelangelo persuaded Pope Julius II to give him a free hand, and proposed a different and more complex scheme, representing the Creation, the Fall of Man, the Promise of Salvation through the prophets, and the genealogy of Christ. The work is part of a larger scheme of decoration within the chapel.

The composition stretches over 500 m^2 of ceiling, and contains over 300 figures. At its center are nine episodes from the Book of Genesis, divided into three groups: God's creation of the earth; God's creation of humankind and their fall from God's grace; and lastly, the state of humanity as represented by Noah and his family. On the pendentives supporting the ceiling are painted twelve men and women who prophesied the coming of Jesus. Among the most famous paintings on the ceiling are The Creation of Adam,

Adam and Eve in the Garden of Eden, the Deluge, the Prophet Jeremiah, and the Cumaean Sibyl.

- 100 years ago, in 1912 - End of the Chinese Empire; Republic of China was established.

USA, New York, from Times Square: W 44th St, looking southeast, with Virgil's Real Barbecue restaurant (center red), MetLife Building (center back).

Chapter 8. 2013 - 2018

2013 –

- 2300th anniversary of the birth of Archimedes (287 BC – 212 BC, aged 75), important Greek mathematician. At 17, in 270 BC, Archimedes, after discovering the water buoyancy theories, said Eureka! In 269 BC, Archimedes, 18, traveled to Alexandria to study – in the same year he invented π. After 6 years, in 263 BC, Archimedes, 24, returned to Syracuse. His inventions Archimedes Claw (213 BC), screw (265 BC), and water buoyancy theories, are developed between 270 BC and 213 BC, when he was 17 to 74. 137 years after the death of Archimedes, in 75 BC, Marcus Tullius Cicero (3 Jan 106 BC – 7 Dec 43 BC, aged 63.9, Roman statesman, orator, and philosopher, who served as consul in the year 63 BC) discovered and restored Archimedes' tomb.

4 March – 100 years ago, Thomas Woodrow Wilson, who was a Professor, was inaugurated as the 28th President of the United States, from 1913 to 1921.

USA, March 2013, Washington: Woodrow Wilson International Center for Scholars (1968) – the author (69.3) at the 1913 Centennial, in celebration of the 100th anniversary of President Woodrow Wilson's inauguration. He was born in Virginia, at Staunton, on 28 December 1856, and died on 3 Feb 1924, aged 67.1.

- 5 October - 300th anniversary of the birth of Denis Diderot (5 Oct 1713 – 31 July 1784, aged 70.8, French philosopher and write).

- 9 October – 200th anniversary of the birth of Giuseppe Verdi (9 October 1813 – 27 January 1901, aged 87.2). He was born at family's home, the first child of Carlo Giuseppe Verdi, 28, (1785 – 1867, aged 82, innkeeper) and Luigia Uttini Verdi, 26, (1787 – 1851, aged 64, spinner), in Le Roncole (90 km southeast of Milano, 90 km southwest of Verona, and 400 km northwest of Roma), a village 4 km southeast of Busseto, then in the Département Taro, which was a part of the First French Empire under Napoléon Bonaparte, 44.1, (15 August 1769 – 5 May 1821, aged 51.7, Emperor of the French 18 May 1804 – 6 April 1814, King of Italy

17 March 1805 – 11 April 1814, Coronation on 26 May 1805 at Milan Cathedral), after the annexation of the Duchy of Parma and Piacenza in 1808.

Japan, north-west of the Sendai Station (1887), on Ekimae Dori, the restaurant Rigoletto, named after the famous opera with the same name, by Giuseppe Verdi (1813 – 1901), who wrote 37 operas, Rigoletto being the 17th, with the premiere at Teatro La Fenice, Venezia, on 11 March 1851.

2014 –

- 400 years ago, in 1614, John Napier, 64, (1550 – 4 April 1617, aged 67; Scottish mathematician, physicist, and astronomer. His Latinized name was Ioannes Neper) published Mirifici Logarithmorum Canonis Descriptio, the first table of logarithms.

2015 –

- 2600th anniversary of the birth of Anaximenes of Miletus, (585 BC - 528 BC, age 57), 15 years older than Pythagoras (Anaximenes died when Pythagoras was 42), Greek philosopher and mathematician.

- 600ᵗʰ anniversary of the birth of Piero della Francesca (c. 1415 – 12 October 1492, aged 77), Italian painter and mathematician. His painting is characterized by its serene humanism, its use of geometric forms and perspective. His most famous work is the cycle of frescoes The History of the True Cross in the church of San Francesco in the Tuscan town of Arezzo. Piero della Francesca had made a detailed study of perspective, and was the first painter to make a scientific study of light. These studies and Alberti's treatise De Pictura were to have a profound effect on younger artists and in particular on Leonardo's own observations and artworks.

- 2 November – 200ᵗʰ anniversary of the birth of George Boole (2 November 1815 – 8 December 1864, aged 49.1), English mathematician, philosopher and logician, the first professor of mathematics at Queen's College, Cork, in Ireland. He worked in the fields of differential equations and algebraic logic, and is best known as the author of The Laws of Thought (1854), which contains Boolean algebra. Boolean logic is the foundation for computers and the information age.

- 19 December – 500 years ago, in 1515, Leonardo, 63.6 years old, was present at the meeting of the King of France Francis I, 21.2 years old, and Pope Leo X, 40, which took place in Bologna, Italy.

- 300 years ago, in 1715, Benjamin Franklin was 9, and had his final formal year of schooling, at Boston Latin School.

USA, Boston, 3 Dec 2009, from Avenue Louis Pasteur (1822-1895, French microbiologist), Boston Public Latin School (1635, Schola Latina Bostoniensis, the oldest and the first public exam school in the U.S.).

2016 –

2400th anniversary of the birth of Aristotle (384 BC – 2 Oct 322 BC, aged 62), great Greek philosopher and scientist, student of Plato (43 years older than Aristotle), teacher of Alexander the Great (20 July 356 BC – 10 June 323 BC, aged 32 years 10 months and 21 days, 28 years younger than Aristotle; Alexander's empire was the largest state of its time, covering approximately 5.2 millions of km^2 (Greece, Turkey, Iraq, Iran, Afghanistan, Pakistan and half of Egypt (which is more than half of the U.S.))).

2017 –

- 20 January - Donald John Trump, 70.6, (born 14 June 1946, at the end of 2018 he was 72.50 was inaugurated as the 45th President of the United States. Before entering politics, he was a businessman and television personality. Trump was born and raised in the New York City borough of Queens.

October – 100 years ago, in 1917, the Russian Revolution ends the Russian Empire; beginning of Russian Civil War.

15 November - at a Christie's auction in New York, Leonardo da Vinci's painting Salvator Mundi (finished by him in 1500, when he was 48) was sold, after 517 years, for a world record of $450.3 M, the highest price ever paid for a work of art.

- 16 November - 300th anniversary of the birth of Jean-Baptiste le Rond d'Alembert (16 November 1717 – 29 October 1783, aged 65.9), French mathematician, mechanician, physicist, philosopher, and music theorist. Until 1759 he was also co-editor with Denis Diderot of the Encyclopédie. D'Alembert's formula for obtaining solutions to the d'Alembert's (wave) equation is named after him.

- 14 December – After 2009 years, Rome city council overturned banishment of 'one of the greatest poets', after Augustus forced him to leave on the year 8 AD. Therefore, 2009 years after Augustus banished him to Tomis, on the Black Sea (now Constanța, Romania), the poet Ovidius has been rehabilitated.
Rome city council on Thursday, 14 Dec 2017, unanimously approved a motion tabled by the M5S party to "repair the serious wrong" suffered by Ovidius, thought of as one of the three canonical poets of Latin literature, along with Vergilius and Horatius.
Best known for his 15-book epic narrative poem Metamorphoses, and the elegy Ars Amatoria, or the Art of Love, Publius Ovidius Naso was exiled in 8 AD to Tomis, the ancient Black Sea settlement now known as the Romanian port city of Constanța.
He remained there until his death, about 9 years later. Although ordered directly by the emperor, scholars have long speculated over the motive for Ovidius' exile; the poet himself attributed it to "carmen et error", a poem and a mistake.
Experts believe the cause was probably a combination of three factors: that Ovidius' erotic poetry was considered offensive, his attitude to Augustus was too disrespectful, and that he may have

been involved in an unspecified plot or scandal. In my view, the reason is that Ovidius was close to Augustus's family, especially to grandson Agrippa Postumus, now 20 and exiled for antisocial behavior, to granddaughter Julia the Younger, 27, also banished (for having an affair with a senator), and to her husband Lucius Aemilius Paullus (37 BC – 8, aged 45), who was executed as a conspirator in a plot against Augustus – it seems that Ovidius new about this plot, but did not inform Augustus.

Sulmona, the Abruzzo town where the poet was born (then Sulmo), formally acquitted him of any wrongdoing. Dante Alighieri (30 May 1265, Firenze, Italy – 14 Sep 1321, Ravenna, Italy, aged 56.3), the great Renaissance poet, was similarly pardoned, after 706 years, in 2008 by Firenze (Florence) – from where he was exiled on pain of death in 1302 (he was 37).

2018 –

- 6 January – U.S. Senator Dr. Rand Paul is 55 years old (born 7 Jan 1963, physician).

- 2 March - Mikhail Gorbachev is 87 years old, president of the International Foundation for Socio-Economic and Political Studies. (born 2 March 1931). He was the eighth and last leader of the Soviet Union, having been General Secretary of the governing Communist Party of the Soviet Union from 1985 until 1991.

- 14 June – The U.S. President Donald Trump is 72 years old.

- 15 June – the Chinese President Xi Jinping is 65 years old (born 15 June 1953, married with Peng Liyuan (55, singer)); he is also general secretary of the Communist Party of China (CPC) Central Committee, and chairman of the Central Military Commission.

- 17 June - Dr. Newt Gingrich is 75 years old (born 17 June 1943), former Speaker.

- 28 July – 1030 years ago, in 988, Volodymyr I of Kiev embraces Christianity, which becomes national religion – it is called Baptism of Rus, and its 1030th anniversary was celebrated in Moscow on 28 July 2018.

- 7 October – the Russian President Vladimir Putin is 66 years old (born 7 Oct 1952, divorced, 2 children).

- 6 November – the author is 75.

- 9 November – 200 years ago, in 1818 – birth of Ivan Turgenev (9 Nov 1818, Oryol (325 km southwest of Moscow), Russia – 3 Sep 1883, Bougival (15 km west of Paris, 6 km north of Versailles), France, aged 64.8, Russian novelist, poet, playwright and translator). On 9 Nov, the 200th anniversary his birth was celebrated in Russia, France and other countries.

- 11 November – in Paris, France, took place a commemorative ceremony marking the centenary of Armistice Day – marking the end of World War I, on 11 November 1918.

- 5 December - 85th anniversary of Prohibition being officially repealed, in 1933, ending the U.S.'s failed experiment in banning alcohol.

11 December – 100th anniversary of the birth of Alexander Solzhenitsyn – a bronze monument, sitting on a granite pedestal, was unveiled in Moscow, in the presence of the Russian President. Aleksandr Isayevich Solzhenitsyn (11 December 1918 – 3 August 2008, aged 89.7) was a Russian novelist, historian, and short story writer. He was an outspoken critic of the Soviet Union and communism, and helped to raise global awareness of its Gulag forced labor camp system.

16 December – in Egypt, in the Saqqara region, which is south of Cairo, a circa 4,460-year-old well-preserved tomb (10 m by 3 m by 3 m) was discovered, which is the final resting place of a royal priest Wahtye, who served during Egypt's Fifth Dynasty (circa 2500 BC to 2350 BC, for 150 years) under the 3rd Pharaoh Neferirkare (Reign circa 2483 BC – 2465 BC, for 18 years). It contains two levels filled with dozens of statues and colorful drawings of the priest and his family, and it is in near-perfect condition. Its drawings are almost completely preserved, and the tomb itself had not been looted, according to Reuters.

21 December – the French President Emmanuel Macron is 41 years old (born 21 Dec 1977, studied philosophy).

24 December - one of the world's most famous Christmas carols, "Silent Night," marks its 200th anniversary on Christmas Eve, 2018.

USA, Cape Cod: A monument at the southwest of Provincetown: The first landing Place of the Pilgrims on November 11, 1620, erected in 1917.

Bibliography

"The Histories" by Polybius
"Discours de la Méthode" by René Descartes
"Meditationes de prima philosophia" by René Descartes
"Philosophiae Naturalis Principia Mathematica" by Isaac Newton
Chinese encyclopedia Gujin Tushu Jicheng (Imperial Enciclopaedia)
"Encyclopédie" by Jean-Baptiste le Rond d'Alembert and Denis Diderot
"Encyclopaedia Britannica" by over 4,400 contributors
"Encyclopedia Americana" by Francis Lieber
"Grand Larousse encyclopédique en 24 volumes" by Albert Ducrocq
"Great Russian Encyclopedia" by Yury Osipov
"Encyclopedia of China"
"Enciclopedia Italiana di Scienze, Lettere ed Arti" (35 volume), by Giovanni Treccani
"Allgemeine Encyclopädie der Wissenschaften und Künste" by Johann Samuel Ersch und Johann Gottfried Gruber
"Gran Enciclopedia de España"

Michael M. Dediu is also the author of these books (which can be found on Amazon.com):

1. Aphorisms and quotations – with examples and explanations
2. Axioms, aphorisms and quotations – with examples and explanations
3. 100 Great Personalities and their Quotations
4. Professor Petre P. Teodorescu – A Great Mathematician and Engineer
5. Professor Ioan Goia – A Dedicated Engineering Professor
6. Venice (Venezia) – a new perspective. A short presentation with photographs
7. La Serenissima (Venice) - a new photographic perspective. A short presentation with many photos

8. Grand Canal – Venice. A new photographic viewpoint. A short presentation with many photos
9. Piazza San Marco – Venice. A different photographic view. A short presentation with many photos
10. Roma (Rome) - La Città Eterna. A new photographic view. A short presentation with many photos
11. Why is Rome so Fascinating? A short presentation with many photos
12. Rome, Boston and Helsinki. A short photographic presentation
13. Rome and Tokyo – two captivating cities. A short photographic presentation
14. Beautiful Places on Earth – A new photographic presentation
15. From Niagara Falls to Mount Fuji via Rome - A novel photographic presentation
16. From the USA and Canada to Italy and Japan - A fresh photographic presentation
17. Paris – Why So Many Call This City Mon Amour - A lovely photographic presentation
18. The City of Light – Paris (La Ville-Lumière) - A kaleidoscopic photographic presentation
19. Paris (Lutetia Parisiorum) – the romance capital of the world - A kaleidoscopic photographic view
20. Paris and Tokyo – a joyful photographic presentation. With a preamble about the Universe
21. From USA to Japan via Canada – A cheerful photographic documentary
22. 200 Wonderful Places, In The Last 50 Years – A personal photographic documentary
23. Must see places in USA and Japan - A kaleidoscopic photographic documentary
24. Grandeurs of the World - A kaleidoscopic photographic documentary
25. Corneliu Leu – writer on the same wavelength as Mark Twain. An American viewpoint
26. From Berkeley to Pompeii via Rome – A kaleidoscopic photographic documentary
27. From America to Europe via Japan - A kaleidoscopic photographic documentary
28. Discover America and Japan - A photographic documentary

29. J. R. Lucas – philosopher on a creative parallel with Plato, An American viewpoint
30. From America to Switzerland via France - A photographic documentary
31. From Bretton Woods to New York via Cape Cod - A photographic documentary
32. Splendid Places on the Atlantic Coast of the U. S. A. - A photographic documentary
33. Fourteen nice Cities on three Continents - A photographic documentary
34. 17 Picturesque Cities on the World Map - A photographic documentary
35. Unforgettable Places from Four Continents including Trump buildings - A photographic documentary
36. Dediu Newsletter, Volume 1, Number 1, 6 December 2016 – Monthly news, review, comments and suggestions for a better and wiser world
37. Dediu Newsletter, Volume 1, Number 2, 6 January 2017 (available at www.derc.com).
38. Dediu Newsletter, Volume 1, Number 3, 6 February 2017 (available at www.derc.com).
39. London and Greenwich, A photographic documentary
40. Dediu Newsletter, Volume 1, Number 4, 6 March 2017 (available also at www.derc.com).
41. Dediu Newsletter, Volume 1, Number 5, 6 April 2017 (available also at www.derc.com).
42. Dediu Newsletter, Volume 1, Number 6, 6 May 2017 (available also at www.derc.com).
43. Dediu Newsletter, Volume 1, Number 7, 6 June 2017 (available also at www.derc.com).
44. London, Oxford and Cambridge, A photographic documentary
45. Dediu Newsletter, Volume 1, Number 8, 6 July 2017 (available also at www.derc.com).
46. Dediu Newsletter, Volume 1, Number 9, 6 August 2017 (available also at www.derc.com).
47. Dediu Newsletter, Volume 1, Number 10, 6 September 2017 (available also at www.derc.com).

48. Three Great Professors: President Woodrow Wilson, Historian Germán Arciniegas, Mathematician Gheorghe Vrănceanu, A chronological and photographic documentary
49. Dediu Newsletter, Volume 1, Number 11, 6 October 2017 (available also at www.derc.com).
50 Dediu Newsletter, Volume 1, Number 12, 6 November 2017 (available also at www.derc.com).
51 Dediu Newsletter, Volume 2, Number 1 (13), 6 December 2017 (available also at www.derc.com).
52 Two Great Leaders: Augustus and George Washington, A chronological and photographic documentary
53. Dediu Newsletter, Volume 2, Number 2 (14), 6 January 2018 (available also at www.derc.com).
54. Newton, Benjamin Franklin, and Gauss, A chronological and photographic documentary
55. Dediu Newsletter, Volume 2, Number 3 (15), 6 February 2018 (available also at www.derc.com).
56. 2017: World Top Events, But Many Little Known, A chronological and photographic documentary
57. Dediu Newsletter, Volume 2, Number 4 (16), 6 March 2018 (available also at www.derc.com).
58. Vergilius, Horatius, Ovidius, and Shakespeare, A chronological and photographic documentary.
59. Dediu Newsletter, Volume 2, Number 5 (17), 6 April 2018 (available also at www.derc.com).
60. Dediu Newsletter, Volume 2, Number 6 (18), 6 May 2018 (available also at www.derc.com).
61. Vivaldi, Bach, Mozart, and Verdi, A chronological and photographic documentary
62. Dediu Newsletter, Volume 2, Number 7 (19), 6 June 2018 (available also at www.derc.com).
63. Dediu Newsletter, Volume 2, Number 8 (20), 6 July 2018 (available also at www.derc.com).
64. Dediu Newsletter, Volume 2, Number 9 (21), 6 August 2018 (available also at www.derc.com).
65. World History, a new perspective - A chronological and photographic documentary.
66. World Humor History with over 100 Jokes, a new perspective - A chronological and photographic documentary

67. Dediu Newsletter, Vol 2, N 10 (22), 6 September 2018
68. Dediu Newsletter, Vol 2, N 11 (23), 6 October 2018
69. Dediu Newsletter, Vol 2, N 12 (24), 6 November 2018
70. Da Vinci, Michelangelo, Rembrandt, Rodin - A chronological and photographic documentary
71. Dediu Newsletter, Vol 3, N 1 (25), 6 December 2018
72. Dediu Newsletter, Vol 3, N 2 (26), 6 January 2019

USA, Bretton Woods: The fire pit and the southeast side of the Mount Washington Resort (1902).

Michael M. Dediu is the editor of these books (also on Amazon.com):

1. Sophia Dediu: The life and its torrents – Ana. In Europe around 1920
2. Proceedings of the 4th International Conference "Advanced Composite Materials Engineering" COMAT 2012
3. Adolf Shvedchikov: I am an eternal child of spring – poems in English, Italian, French, German, Spanish and Russian
4. Adolf Shvedchikov: Life's Enigma – poems in English, Italian and Russian
5. Adolf Shvedchikov: Everyone wants to be HAPPY – poems in English, Spanish and Russian
6. Adolf Shvedchikov: My Life, My Love – poems in English, Italian and Russian
7. Adolf Shvedchikov: I am the gardener of love – poems in English and Russian
8. Adolf Shvedchikov: Amaretta di Saronno – poems in English and Russian
9. Adolf Shvedchikov: A Russian Rediscovers America
10. Adolf Shvedchikov: Parade of Life - poems in English and Russian
11. Adolf Shvedchikov: Overcoming Sorrow - poems in English and Russian
12. Sophia Dediu: Sophia meets Japan
13. Corneliu Leu: Roosevelt, Churchill, Stalin and Hitler: Their surprising role in Eastern Europe in 1944
14. Proceedings of the 5th International Conference "Computational Mechanics and Virtual Engineering" COMEC 2013
15. Georgeta Simion – Potanga: Beyond Imagination: A Thought-provoking novel inspired from mid-20th century events
16. Ana Dediu: The poetry of my life in Europe and The USA
17. Ana Dediu: The Four Graces
18. Proceedings of the 5th International Conference "Advanced Composite Materials Engineering" COMAT 2014
19. Sophia Dediu: Chocolate Cook Book: Is there such a thing as too much chocolate?

20. Sorin Vlase: Mechanical Identifiability in Automotive Engineering
21. Gabriel Dima: The Evolution of the Aerostructures – Concept and Technologies
22. Proceedings of the 6th International Conference "Computational Mechanics and Virtual Engineering" COMEC 2015
23. Sophia Dediu: Cook Book 1 A-B-C Common sense cooking
24. Sophia Dediu: Dim Sum Spring Festival
25. Ana Dediu and Sophia Dediu: Europe in 1985: A chronological and photographic documentary
26 Stefan Staretu: Europe: Serbian Despotate of Srem and the Romanian area. Between the 14th and the 16th Centuries

Italy, Rome (753 BC), Villa Borghese (1630), Lake Garden, from Viale del Lago, Tempio di Esculapio (1786, Temple of Asclepius (god of medicine, healing, rejuvenation and physicians)) on artificial island; on front, in Greek "To Asclepius the savior".

Italy, Roma (753 BC, one of the oldest occupied cities in Europe, called Roma Aeterna (The Eternal City) and Caput Mundi (Capital of the World)), southeast of Piazza del Popolo (1822, by Giuseppe Valadier, inside the northern gate in the Aurelian Walls, the Porta Flaminia, now called the Porta del Popolo), near Via del Babuino (opened in 1525 as the Via Paolina) and the church Santa Maria in Montesanto (1679, begun by Rainaldi and completed by Bernini and Fontana), the statue of the Goddess of Abundance.

www.ingramcontent.com/pod-product-compliance
Lightning Source LLC
Chambersburg PA
CBHW041622220426
43662CB00001B/16